TOWARDS A
THEOLOGY
OF RELIGIONS

Routledge Religious Studies

Advisory Editor: Professor Stewart Sutherland, Principal,
King's College London

TOWARDS A THEOLOGY OF RELIGIONS

GLYN RICHARDS

ROUTLEDGE

LONDON AND NEW YORK

For Russell and Millie

and

in memory of Mary

First published in 1989 by Routledge
11 New Fetter Lane, London EC4P 4EE
29 West 35th Street, New York, NY 10001

© 1989 Glyn Richards

Printed in Great Britain by T J Press (Padstow) Ltd, Padstow, Cornwall

British Library Cataloguing in Publication Data

Richards, Glyn
Towards a theology of religions.
1. Religions.   I. Title.
291

Library of Congress Cataloging in Publication Data

Richards, Glyn
Towards a theology of religions.
Bibliography: p.
Includes index.
1. Christianity and other religions – History.   I. Title.
BR127.R49   1989   261.2   88–26354

ISBN   0 – 415 – 02450 – 1

CONTENTS

CONTENTS

PREFACE

I am indebted to the editor of this series, Stewart R. Sutherland, for inviting me to contribute on the subject of a theology of religions. He was aware of my interest in this field from articles and reviews that I had written from time to time, and I am grateful to him for affording me the opportunity to concentrate my mind on what I have always considered to be an intriguing area of study.

It would not have been possible for me to devote an uninterrupted period of study to do the research necessary for this book had I not been granted sabbatical leave for a semester by the University of Stirling. I am grateful to the University authorities for providing me with the time and opportunity to write this book and to the inter-library loan department for their help in acquiring many of the books I needed.

I am indebted to Ninian Smart and Dewi Phillips for their comments and suggestions; to my academic colleagues for copies of books that were proving elusive; and to my secretary Elspeth Gillespie for sheltering me from unwelcome intrusions on my time. Above all I am indebted to my wife for reading the manuscript, correcting errors, and assisting with the preparation of the index.

Glyn Richards

INTRODUCTION

We are confronted today by the existence of what is often referred to as religious pluralism. In fact, religious pluralism has become something of a stock phrase and there have been quite a number of analyses of, and approaches to, what has been called the pluralistic religious situation of today. It is not at all clear to me in what way the pluralistic religious situation of today differs from the pluralistic religious situation of yesterday. The varieties of religious experiences pertaining today show no substantial increase on, or difference from, those of yesterday. What has occurred over the last century, however, has been a significant growth in the awareness of religious pluralism. There have been references, for example, to the existence of a 'planetary culture', by which is meant, in all probability, the fact that the world has grown smaller as a result of improved communications; that it is no longer possible for a man to confine himself to the small island of his own culture and traditions; and that acknowledgement of the significance and vitality of other cultures and traditions is unavoidable. Reference is also made to the ghetto mentality of those theologians who attempt to work within the confines of their own religious traditions in total isolation from the deep, spiritual insights of other religious traditions. It might be argued, of course, by those who work within the confines of their own traditions and cultures that they can do no other; that it is as participants in a particular form of life that they understand what it is to think and act in accordance with certain cultural, religious and ethical criteria; and that to talk of a 'planetary culture', as if such a phenomenon is somehow self-explanatory, really makes no sense. It might also be argued by those who are accused of cultivating a ghetto mentality that, since religious commitment involves seeking a fuller understanding of the theological implications of the particular religious tradition to which they belong, to talk of a theology of religions is nonsense. It may well be asked, therefore, whether the concept of a theology of religions is as much an abstraction as is the concept of a 'planetary culture', and whether it makes more sense to talk about theologies of religions rather than a theology of religions. Are we not confronted with different cultures in the world rather than a 'planetary culture'? And does it not make more sense to talk of a *Christian* theology of religions, or a *Hindu, Buddhist,* or an *Islamic* theology of religions rather than such an abstraction as a theology of religions, as if such a theology could be constructed in isolation from particular religious traditions?

The significance of these references to a 'planetary culture' and a ghetto mentality, however, ought not to be overlooked. While it may be appropriate to recognize that the endeavour to construct a *Christian* theology of religions, for example, is more meaningful and consequently more acceptable than seeking to define an abstract theology of religions without reference to a particular religious tradition, the danger of ignoring the spiritual insights of religions other than one's own is a very real one for the theologian. Similarly, preoccupation with one's own culture can lead to myopia, which blinds us to the immense richness and diversity of other cultures in the world. In this sense at least the references to a 'planetary culture' and the dangers of a ghetto mentality are salutary.

The purpose of this work is to examine some of the problems involved in seeking to delineate a Christian theology of religions. I shall seek to show how the growing concern with religious plurality has found expression in phenomenological approaches to the study of religion; in different attempts to find what is purported to be the essence of religion; in the search for the common origin of religion; and in the declarations of the Second Vatican Council. I shall endeavour to indicate also how concern for a specifically Christian theology of religions has emerged as a result of increasing acquaintance with the teachings of the major religions of the world and personal encounter with their living representatives.

I shall endeavour to examine in the course of this study some of the different theological responses to religious pluralism that have emerged over the past years including the exclusivist response of theologians like Barth and Kraemer; the inclusivism of Toynbee; the relativism of Troeltsch; the evolutionism, if it can be so described, of certain Catholic theologians; the essentialist approach of theologians like Schleiermacher; the response of upholders of the doctrine of the Logos or the cosmic Christ; and the dialogical approach of modern scholars of religious studies.

The problem of truth claims naturally looms large in any attempt to construct a Christian theology of religions and in seeking a resolution of the problems raised by conflicting truth claims this work will be no exception. Questions of uniqueness, superiority, normativeness and finality inevitably emerge in relation to the Christian understanding of the person of Christ. The existence of alternative claims to uniqueness or finality in other religions lead us inevitably to enquire whether there may be an independent criterion of truth whereby we might adjudicate between competing truth claims. Whether such a search is itself confused is another question and one that recent studies in the philosophy of religion may help us to resolve. What might well emerge from our investigations, however, is the realization that anyone embarking on the task of constructing a Christian theology of religions will not be able to ignore the occurrence of certain features in other religions similar to those for which uniqueness is claimed within his own religious tradition.

Chapter One

CONCERN WITH PLURALITY

The growing concern with religious plurality has found expression in a variety of ways not the least of which has been the phenomenological approach to the study of religion. This approach is comparatively recent and has been referred to as a child of the Enlightenment. It is indicative of a growing awareness of, and interest in, religious diversity, and in the spirit of the Enlightenment seeks to apply scientific methods to the investigation of religious traditions. It strives to promote a neutral, objective, and disinterested approach to the study of religion. To what extent it is possible to succeed in this task is a moot point and has proved to be a recurring theme in methodological discussions. Clearly a scientific, empirical approach to the study of religion has its limitations. It cannot, for example, raise questions concerning the truth or validity of religious truth claims nor make judgements as to their merit or value. If or when it does so it ceases to be a scientific approach to the subject. Those who in the name of scientific investigation or empirical research seek to offer rational grounds for religious belief overstep the limits of their approach. They cease to be scientific or empirical investigators of religious phenomena and instead become empirical philosophers of religion. Perhaps the tendency to move from the phenomenology of religion to the philosophy of religion is a perfectly natural one, yet there are those who would insist that the distinction can and must be maintained and that the methodology of a phenomenological approach to the study of religion is quite autonomous.

Before raising questions concerning the possibility or otherwise of a totally objective, neutral, unbiased approach to the study of religion, it may be appropriate to examine the reasons put forward

1

for maintaining the autonomous nature of the scientific, phenomenological approach to the study of religion. The claim of
phenomenologists is that if the study of religion is to be
academically viable then its subject matter must be open to the
same scientific scrutiny as other fields of study. The science of
religion cannot differ in kind from the scientific investigation of
other subject matters. The aim of the academic study of religion,
therefore, must be to elucidate and clarify religious phenomena
including such features as belief in supernatural beings, cultic
celebrations, doctrinal statements, and ethical behaviour. It may
involve the use of a variety of techniques and depend on the results
achieved in such disciplines as sociology, anthropology, and
history, but basically it seeks to provide knowledge of the
phenomena of different religious traditions. It has been suggested
that there are certain axioms for the academic study of religion of
which the following three are basic:[1]

(i)   that the academic study of religion is a scientific study;
(ii) that as scientific it is essentially critical and analytic;
(iii) that although scientific it is not itself a science or a special
      discipline.

The first axiom disposes of the necessity of religious understanding
or commitment as an a priori for the study of religion. The second
axiom distinguishes between the experiential approach of the
devotee and the phenomenological approach of the student of
religion. The third axiom establishes religious studies as an area
discipline involving the use of various techniques and methods for
the understanding of religious phenomena.

A similar point is made concerning the academic study of
religion when it is suggested that three essential qualities underlie
the discipline. First, that a sympathetic understanding of religions
other than one's own should prevail. Secondly, that we should
adopt an attitude of self-criticism concerning our own religious
background. And thirdly, that we should cultivate the scientific
approach.[2] The cultivation of a scientific approach to the study of
religion emerged, as we have seen, during the Enlightenment and
is referred to by Max Müller as *Religionswissenschaft* (a term used in
the first instance to distinguish the science of religion from the
philosophy of religion and theology) the starting point of which, it
is claimed, is the historically given religions.[3]

2

But to return to the questions posed earlier. Is the science of religion a distinct autonomous discipline and what arguments can be put forward in favour of an objective, neutral, unbiased, phenomenological approach to the study of religion? Do not doubts arise when we ask whether it is possible to be totally neutral, unbiased or 'scientific', or to bring a totally disinterested mind to bear on the investigation of religious beliefs? Is there such a thing as an open-ended, purely objective approach to the study of religion? Are there not, in actual fact, degrees of bias or interest, and would it not be advantageous in the long run to recognize and acknowledge them? Phenomenologists might well admit that while the science of religion, or *Religionswissenschaft*, is an autonomous discipline in the sense that it is not simply a term for a combination of disciplines involved in the study of religion, it depends nevertheless quite heavily on other disciplines, such as the descriptive aspects of history and the analytic accounts of sociology, psychology and anthropology.[4] They might be persuaded to acknowledge also that a totally unbiased, open-ended approach to the study of religion is an impossibility; but they might still wish to draw a distinction between an objective, scientific, phenomeno-logical approach and the a priori notions and preconceptions that determine certain theological or philosophical approaches to religious studies. But is the distinction one of degree rather than of kind? Should the phenomenologist, for example, wish to proceed on the assumption that all religions contain relative rather than absolute truth, could it not be argued that his assumption is as much an a priori notion as the Christian theologian's claim that only Christianity is true and all other religions are false.

It may be the case that the kind of interests exemplified in the phenomenological approach to the study of religion is incompatible with the quest for a theology of religions whether Christian, Hindu, Muslim or Buddhist, since such a quest is an explicitly theological undertaking. This would lead us to look at the question of *Religionswissenschaft* from another angle. We may want to enquire whether religion can really be studied scientifically. Is there not something unique in the experience of faith which makes a scientific, empirical investigation of it impossible? Is not Cantwell Smith's observation relevant here, namely, that a man cannot be 'an observer *vis-à-vis* the history of the diverse religions of distinct or even close communities but rather a participant in the

3

multiform religious history of the only community there is, humanity'?[5] And does not Smith echo Otto, who insists that while a phenomenological approach to the study of religion examines the external expressions of religious experience from without, a true understanding of religion is achieved only from within and consequently demands a theological approach.[6]

To put the question in another form: can one draw a distinction between religious traditions and the faith which finds expression in those traditions? Is it possible to confine the study of religion to a scientific investigation of the phenomenology of religion, or the examination of the truth *about* a religion as distinct from a theological concern with the question of the truth *of* a religion? Does intellectual openness, sometimes regarded as synonymous with a phenomenological approach to the study of religion, necessarily involve ignoring the implications of a theological concern with the truth of religion? Phenomenology, or the science of religion, may be a necessary condition for the apprehension of religious traditions but is it a sufficient condition for the understanding of religious beliefs?

The problem has been expressed in a number of different ways. The integrity of *Religionswissenschaft* as an academic discipline has been questioned by theologians, philosophers, and social scientists formerly attracted to the phenomenological approach to the study of religion. Four main criticisms have been cited by different groups. First, some maintain that historians of religion are really philosophers of religions since all religions are simply manifestations of an underlying primordial religion and that the task of the history of religions is to lead humanity to an awareness of the absolute truth. Second, some claim that the objective approach of *Religionswissenschaft* is not sufficiently objective and phenomeno-logical because of the nature of the subject, and that it should strive to be so with the assistance of cognate disciplines. Third, there are those who insist that insufficient attention is paid to the subjective elements of religions and the importance of allowing the followers of each religion to express their own views about life and the nature of their religious beliefs and experiences. Fourth, there are those who deny the possibility of an objective approach to the study of religions on the grounds that we are all conditioned and determined by our own forms of life and by the religious, ethical, and cultural milieu in which we are nurtured. Hence the need to

4

recognize that the history of religions must be written from a particular religious or theological standpoint, whether it be Christian, Hindu, or Islamic, and irrespective of whether or not *Missionswissenschaft* is ultimately involved. [7]

Aspects of the third criticism find expression in the writings of Wilfred Cantwell Smith. He views the twentieth century as a time of the coming together of people to form one community. The implication of this for the comparative study of religion is the development of a more personalized, realistic approach, and the exploration of the essential human quality of the subject. For Smith the study of religion is above all the study of persons. While it clearly involves the study of tangible externals such as symbols, institutions, doctrines, and practices, it is also the study of human hopes and aspirations. After all, 'Faith is a quality of men's lives' and when we study religion we are concerned with the 'qualities of personal living'.[8] We are making progress in the study of religion when we recognize that we are dealing with people and not with religious systems and 'that no statement about a religion is valid unless it can be acknowledged by that religion's believers'.[9] Smith is at pains to point out that by religion in this context he means the faith in men's hearts. While it may be possible for the academic student of religion to discover much about the externals of a religious system he cannot possibly go beyond the believer when it comes to understanding the significance and meaning that system has for the community of faith. What this implies is that the detached, non-participatory, academic approach to the study of religion has given way to a more personal relationship between the student of religion and the religion he investigates. This encounter fosters dialogue which in turn makes exclusivism and proselytism unacceptable.[10] It is Smith's belief that dialogue between religions may lead in the end 'to reconciliation and to an enlarged sense of community',[11] and when the community becomes sufficiently large, the study of religion in turn becomes a human study 'where scholars of different faiths no longer confront each other but collaborate in jointly confronting the universe, and consider together the problems in which all of them are involved'.[12] This is for Smith the beginning of the movement towards a world theology which he considers to be the ultimate goal for mankind. Not a Christian, Hindu, Buddhist or Muslim theology of religions, but a world theology which seeks 'to interpret intellectually all human faith, one's own and others'; comprehensively and justly . . . seeing one's own group as a component in the total community of humankind. . .'[13] He is able to make this submission because for him faith differs in form and not in kind. As the Christian has been saved by a Christian form of faith, so has their Muslim, Buddhist, Hindu, and Jew been saved by their respective forms and patterns of faith.[14]

Needless to say, advocates of the phenomenological, scientific approach to the study of religion would reject these criticisms on the grounds that if the study of religion is to be truly academic then its methodology must be on a par, or isomorphic, with other sciences. If it is claimed that religion is so esoteric and noumenal as to be the concern of devotees alone then a detached, objective study of religion is out of the question. Phenomenologists would reject this claim, insisting that the scientific approach to the study of religion, even at its simplest level, provides knowledge of the facts about different religious tradition from an objective standpoint. But it goes beyond this when it seeks in inductive fashion, through the use of the various techniques and methods of different disciplines, to understand the nature of religious phenomena and engages in comparative studies.[15] But whatever the arguments for and against the phenomenological approach to the study of religion what can be stated unequivocally is that it is indicative of the current concern with religious pluralism.

Concern for some kind of assessment of religious plurality has also taken the form of a quest for the essence of religion. It may be true to say that Hegel was one of the first to wrestle with the problem of conceptualizing religion and hence may well be regarded as the forerunner of those who consider religion to be a self-subsisting essence, a transcendental entity preceding all historical manifestations, a prototype, as it were, of all particular, socio-historical instances. Not all would approve the explicit ascription of this idea to Hegel, but there are those who would maintain that he does conceive of religion as 'a *Begriff*, a self-subsisting transcendent idea that unfolds itself in dynamic expression in the course of everchanging history, unfolds itself as "positive religion" (in the singular)'.[16] It might be argued that as an idealist and a monist who considers reality to be one, he views all particulars as differentiations of the absolute spirit and, as such, capable of being fully comprehended only in their relation to the whole, the absolute

6

spirit. To understand the particular fully it is necessary to penetrate beyond its manifestation to the universal whole, or essential unity, of which it is an aspect and which it portrays. Religion, it might be said, represents or pictures the absolute spirit or mind while philosophy conceives or thinks it. Particular, historical religions portray in varying degrees the absolute unity or whole that religion represents or pictures. They are particular manifestations of the pictorially presented absolute spirit or whole.[17]

Schleiermacher also conceives of religion as pre-existing individual, historical manifestations. He sees particular religions as being grounded in the fundamental unity of religion, an a priori condition. The transcendental unity of religion is necessary for the existence of positive, historical religions which are the concrete expressions of the primordial form, the immediate religious consciousness, 'the sense and taste for the infinite'. No limited, finite, positive form of religion can encapsulate the universality or infinitude of religion. The notion that a single, finite form of religion can be universally valid is inappropriate.[18] But it does not follow that finite forms are superfluous and that all we need is a kind of natural religion. Religion has to find expression in concrete forms and the plurality of particular religions is necessary for the complete manifestation of religion. Antipathy to religious pluralism should be avoided. Each positive religion, according to Schleiermacher, contains something of the true nature of religion, and the primordial form, the essence, or the transcendental unity of religion, is comprehended not by deducing it from the common elements of particular religions as a kind of abstraction, but in and through the language of particular religions. Particular religions are true in so far as they succeed in expressing the primordial form of religion, which in turn is comprehended only in the depths of particular religions.[19]

But is it possible to maintain the existence of a primordial element which is the essence of all particular religions and the transcendental unity underlying them? How do we isolate such an element or apprehend the essence or transcendental unity of religion? And how do we go about determining the truth of particular religions by means of this primordial element? How does one distinguish, for example, between different degrees or grades of numinosity? Is it possible that the quest for the essence of religion simply leads us further away from a true understanding of religious traditions? Cantwell Smith seems to think that that is precisely the case. Our inability to define the term 'religion' adequately, he maintains, indicates that we should drop it altogether since it does not correspond to an existing entity which can be determined.[20] He describes it further as 'confusing, unnecessary, and distorting', and not something 'that can be formulated and externalized into an observable pattern theoretically abstractible from the persons who live it'.[21] Whether the failure to define the term religion adequately is a sufficient reason for dropping it altogether is another matter and highly debatable. It is only when the term religion is used to refer to a transcendental essence, or entity, that difficulties arise. When it is used to refer to a particular religious tradition the same difficulties do not apply. Smith correctly cites Barth as one of the foremost antagonists of the concept of religion and considers it surprising that we should even want to regard religion as the Aristotelean essence of all particulars as if particular instances must of necessity have a common element.[22] This is not to deny that there may be a great deal of common ground, or what might be called family resemblances between religions. But to admit that is a far cry from claiming that there is a primordial element common to all particular religions which can be called the transcendental unity of religion. As Smith points out, there are problems in seeking to postulate 'a transcendental ideal of which the historical actualities are a succession of mundane and therefore imperfect, compromised manifestations'.[23] In place of the term religion, Smith would substitute the twin concepts of faith and cumulative tradition, i.e. the religious experience of people, on the one hand, and the historical data of the religious life of people on the other. The latter he considers to be a human construct; it is the *expression* of faith and can take many forms. The former he conceives to be the impingement of the transcendent on the lives of people. What we call religion then, according to Smith, is not a primordial element, or essence, or transcendental unity, but the dialectical process or interaction between tradition and faith.[24] The question that arises is what is meant by the phrase 'impingement of the transcendent' and whether its use raises difficulties for Smith similar to those that he is criticizing in relation to essence and the notion of transcendental unity.

But whatever the arguments for and against the quest for the essence or transcendental unity of religion, it is a further indication of an awareness of, and interest in, religious diversity, and the current concern with religious pluralism.

Concern with religious plurality is also implicit if not explicit in the declarations of the Second Vatican Council of the Roman Catholic Church, 1963–5. In the declaration *Lumen Gentiun*, dated 21 November 1964, it is stated that

> Those who, through no fault of their own, do not know the Gospel of Christ or his Church, but who nevertheless seek God with a sincere heart, and, moved by grace, try in their actions to do his will as they know it through the dictates of their conscience – those too may achieve eternal salvation.[25]

The same applies to those who without explicit knowledge of God endeavour to live a good life. This is a step forward, albeit a tentative one, from the clear pronouncement of Pope Pius IX in 1854, which takes the form:

> It is to be held by faith that outside the apostolic Roman Church no one can be saved; it is the only ark of salvation and anyone who does not enter it will perish in the flood. But it is also to be considered certain that those who labour under invincible ignorance of the true religion are not guilty of this matter in the eyes of the Lord.[26]

The declaration of the Second Vatican Council might be regarded as confirmation of the anti-Jansenist pronouncement of the Church which might be expressed positively as *extra ecclesiam conceditur gratia*. But if it is conceded that there is divine grace *extra ecclesiam* and yet no salvation *extra ecclesiam*, how are these two pronouncements to be reconciled? If the declaration of the second Vatican Council is to make sense, and if the pronouncement of Pope Pius IX is not to stand out like a sore thumb in the new theological context of post-Vatican II, then clearly some non-exclusive interpretation of the statement that *extra ecclesiam salus non est* would seem to be required. One attempt at such an interpretation is the suggestion that *extra ecclesiam salus non est* refers to a 'principle defining a category' and not 'a principle concerning persons' and that if people are saved by divine grace, they are saved because of the representative capacity of the Church, that is to say, the

9

Church represents God's grace.[27] I must admit that the logic of this interpretation put forward by Schlette escapes me. But even if we were to grant its validity, questions relating to the Church's teaching concerning the necessity of the sacraments of baptism and the eucharist for salvation, and whether the saving grace of the Church works retrospectively, would still need to be answered. If the sacraments are essential for salvation, in what sense are they to be regarded as essential in view of the possibility of eternal salvation through grace for those non-Christians who, according to the declaration of Vatican II, strive to do God's will as revealed to them through their conscience? That is, in what sense are sacraments essential if salvation is available through grace for those who strive to do God's will by living in accordance with high ethical principles, and where morality is considered somehow to take the place of baptism?[28] It is evident that consideration of such questions and problems are not unrelated to the formulation of a Christian theology of religions.

The declaration of the Second Vatican Council on the relation of the Church to non-Christian religions is dated 28 October 1965, and entitled *Nostra Aetate*. It recognizes the duty of the Church to promote unity and fellowship among nations and peoples, and acknowledges that men look to different religions for an answer to the problems of existence. The Catholic Church, it states, does not reject anything that is true and holy in these religions; often their doctrines reflect a ray of that truth which enlightens all men. Yet at the same time the Church is compelled to proclaim Christ as the way, the truth, and the life. While witnessing to their own faith, therefore, Christians should enter into dialogue with non-Christians and seek to encourage the spiritual and moral truths embodied in their religious life and culture. Hinduism explores the divine mystery, expressing it through the riches of myth and philosophical insights. Buddhism testifies to the inadequacy of the changing world. Muslims worship the merciful and almighty God who is Creator of heaven and earth and submit themselves to his decrees. Dissensions may have arisen in the past, but they must be set aside and every effort made to promote mutual understanding. Christians and Jews share a common spiritual heritage and though the Church is the new people of God, the Jews should not be spoken of as rejected or accursed, and mutual understanding and appreciation must be encouraged. All men are created in the image of God, and our relation to our fellow men and to God are dependent on one another. The Church reproves, therefore, discrimination or harassment of people on the grounds of race, colour, or religion as alien to the mind of Christ.[29]

The declaration is referred to as a milestone in the history of the relationship between Christians and Jews. It provides the opportunity for dialogue which had been prevented in the past by mutual ignorance. All forms of anti-Semitism are condemned and Christians urged to seek a better knowledge of the religious traditions of Judaism and to promote dialogue. This does not mean that the Church should cease to proclaim Christ to the world, but it must do so while, at the same time, showing respect for religious liberty. The common elements in Jewish and Christian liturgies, and the continuity of the Christian faith with that of the earlier Covenant, should be recognized in order that better relations might be established, for 'the very return of Christians to the sources and origins of their faith, grafted on to the earlier Covenant, helps the search for unity in Christ, the corner-stone.'[30]

The uniqueness of the Christian revelation is made clear in the declaration of the Second Vatican Council entitled *Dei Verbum* and dated 18 November 1965. Through divine revelation God manifests himself and makes known his will for the salvation of mankind. The fullness of the revelation of God is to be found in Christ who commanded his apostles to proclaim the Gospel, which in turn becomes the source of all saving truth. Apostolic preaching is preserved in the tradition and scriptures of the Church which together constitute 'the single sacred deposit of the Word of God'.[31]

The question that naturally poses itself here is, what is the relation of the unique revelation of God through Christ to the general revelation of God to mankind through other religions, the doctrines of which, we are told, often reflect a ray of that truth which enlightens all men? There does not seem to be a specific reference to the concept of general revelation, although, as we have noted, the Catholic Church is at pains to point out that it does not reject anything that is true and holy in non-Christian religions. As far as the missionary work of the Church is concerned the message of Vatican II is specific and uncompromising. The declaration *Ad Gentes Divinitus* dated 7 December 1965, refers to the Church as having been sent to be 'the universal sacrament of salvation'.[32] It is, by its very nature, missionary, because it has been sent by

11

Christ to reveal the love of God to all men. Countless millions of people have never heard the Gospel message and among them are those who belong to one or other of the great religions of the world. If the Church is to be in a position to reveal the love of God and offer men salvation 'then it must implant itself among all these groups in the same way that Christ by his incarnation committed himself to the particular social and cultural circumstance of the men among whom he lived'.[33] As Christ, through dialogue, led men to the divine light, so too should his disciples converse with those they live with that they might learn of the Gospel. The same specific message is to be found in the declaration *Evangelii nuntiandi*, dated 8 December 1975. The Church, it is stated, has been entrusted with the proclamation of the Gospel which might take the form of a silent but effective witness to values which transcend ordinary values, and which would manifest themselves in the way Christians live their lives. This might be considered to be a first step in the work of evangelization, since it might lead non-Christians, among whom would be those who seek something or someone whom they cannot identify, to ask why Christians live the way they do. This in turn could lead to further questions of a deeper and more profound nature.[34] The proclamation of the Gospel is relevant also for those followers of non-Christian religions in whom the spiritual life has found valid expression, and who have sought God sincerely, though imperfectly. Like others they have the right to know the riches of the mystery of Christ.[35]

Whatever we may think of the success or failure of the declarations of the Second Vatican Council *vis-à-vis* other religions, there can be no doubt that they show an awareness of religious diversity and express a concern for the implications of religious plurality for the message of the Church.

Concern with religious pluralism has been evident also in the writings of many theologians as a result of their increasing acquaintance with the major religions of the world. This is true, for example, of Paul Tillich. Mircea Eliade refers to his *reawakened* interest in the history of religions as a result of his visit to Japan in 1960 and his encounter with living representatives of Buddhism and Shinto.[36] The term 'reawakened' is apposite, because his initial attraction to the history of religions was during his student days when his teacher, Martin Kähler, showed him the perils of doctrinal narrowness and exclusivism with the loss of openness and spiritual freedom that ensued,[37] and when acquaintance with the work of Jacob Boehme and Ernst Troeltsch revealed to him the mystical, social and historical aspects of religion. It was Troeltsch who first showed him the value of religious cross-fertilization which, together with Rudolf Otto's analysis of the structure of the holy, helped him to formulate his dynamic-typological approach to the history of religions, in which the three main elements of religion, namely, the sacramental, mystical, and prophetic, are analysed and compared.[38] We shall examine this approach in greater detail later, together with the contribution of Troeltsch and Otto to the understanding of religious plurality. We shall discuss also the exclusivist approach of Karl Barth, Emil Brunner, and Hendrik Kraemer, and the inclusivist approach of Arnold Toynbee, all of whom showed their concern in different ways with the religious pluralism with which they were confronted.

The same concern with religious plurality is to be found in the works of Catholic theologians, of whom Karl Rahner is an eminent example. He describes today's pluralistic situation as qualitatively new and an insurmountable fact. A similar concern is expressed in the work of John Hick who, somewhat picturesquely, describes today's pluralism as representing a revolution from a Ptolemaic religion-centred situation to a Copernican God-centred situation.[39] The contributions of Rahner and his fellow Catholic theologians, and the dialogical approach to world religions of John Hick and others, will be examined in subsequent chapters.

Chapter Two

THE NEO-ORTHODOX RESPONSE: BARTH, BRUNNER, KRAEMER

The interest in religious diversity and concern with the problems of religious pluralism which we have referred to find expression in a variety of theological responses on the part of Christians to the existence of different religious traditions. One response might be called exclusivist and its primary characteristic is that it draws a sharp distinction between faith and religion. The favourable attitude that had previously been shown towards the history and plurality of religions suffered a reverse in the early decades of the twentieth century as a consequence of the exclusivism of the prevailing theological climate. Tillich, for example, refers to the sense of theological isolation experienced by his friends Rudolf Otto and Friedrich Heiler, and of the attacks levelled against his own views during a seminar on Schleiermacher held at Marburgh.[1] The neo-orthodox attitude that prevailed at the time, and which is primarily associated with the name of Karl Barth, referred to faith as man's response to God's self-revelation in his Word, which was incarnate in Christ, contained in Scripture, and proclaimed in the Church, and to religion as man's arrogant and futile attempt to attain to knowledge of God by his own efforts. It could be regarded as a modern version of the older orthodox attitude that distinguished between *vera religio* and *religiones falsae*. The issue is a simple one of distinguishing between revelation on the one hand, and religion on the other, or between revealed theology and natural theology. The point of the distinction is to make it perfectly clear that the revelation in Christ is not to be regarded as an extension of natural religion but rather a direct consequence of the gracious activity of God. The emphasis is placed on discontinuity rather than continuity and on the radical displacement of other religions by the Christian faith.

As the foremost representative of this viewpoint Barth defines religion as unbelief. At best, he maintains, it is indicative of man's perverted response to God's initiative and at worst it is a manifestation of man's deliberate revolt against God. The Church, he claims, is the locus of faith or that which might possibly be termed religion in the true sense of the term. This is the case, however, not because of a process of differentiation conducted on the basis of an analysis of the general concept of religion, but rather as a consequence of God's self-revelation through his grace. Like a man who is justified, true religion is a creature of grace. It is never true in and of itself; it can only become true through grace. Of itself it must be understood simply as man's attempt to come to knowledge of God by means of his own efforts and is therefore in direct contradiction to revelation, which is God's self-manifestation through grace. It cannot even be interpreted as man's attempt to co-operate with God, as if it could in some way be regarded as man's appropriation of God's grace in revelation. Religion is really man's substitute for revelation. It cannot provide knowledge of God. There is no continuity between religion and revelation; the one radically displaces the other. Only when religion is justified or sanctified by revelation can it be considered to be true. The truth of the Christian religion, therefore, is related not to the fact that it is fundamentally superior to other religions, but rather to the fact that it is the consequence of revelatory grace. The Church is the locus of true religion only in so far as it exists and lives by grace.[2]

According to Barth, revelation is the act whereby God reconciles man to himself through grace. It presupposes that man is incapable of reconciling himself to God, or declaring himself righteous, because of his fallen state. Man is justified and sanctified once and for all through the revelation of God in Christ. For man to know that he is incapable of saving himself requires a revelatory act and this knowledge also is imparted through Christ. Faith then consists in recognizing, admitting, affirming, and accepting the fact that everything has been done for us in Christ. This is a further illustration, in Barth's view, of the distinction that has to be drawn between revelation and religion.

Can we infer from this that Barth regards Christianity as the true faith or true religion and other non-Christian religions as false? On the face of it the argument seems to point in that direction, but as we have seen he insists that the Christian religion is true only in so far as it listens to divine revelation and recognizes religion as unbelief. That is, a distinction has to be drawn between religion and faith. If Christianity assumes that the definition of religion as unbelief applies only to non-Christian religions and not to Christianity itself as a religion, then it fails to understand the discontinuity that exists between revelation and religion. If Christianity assumes that as a religion it occupies a position of privilege among the religions of the world, then it has already forfeited its claim to be the locus of faith. The Christian religion, as much as non-Christian religions, stands under the judgement of unbelief pronounced on all manifestations of religion. The Church must never forsake its belief in the sufficiency of God's grace, nor must it seek to resist other religions by appealing to religious experience or religious self-consciousness. Its truth does not rest on its inherent holiness, or its religious self-consciousness, or religious experience (an implicit criticism of Schleiermacher), but in the knowledge of God's grace and revelation through faith.[3]

It could be argued that Barth is providing the Church with a salutary reminder of its status. But the question that arises is, what is one to make of the claim of other religions, or the faiths of other men, that God reveals himself to them also in an act of grace? Is Ramakrishna mistaken when he claims to have had visions of God at Dakshineshwar and are his followers mistaken and misguided when they refer to him as God-intoxicated and a God-inspired mystic? Is Barth here presenting us with an example of theological positivism, as Bonhoeffer calls it, comparable with the philosophical positivism of the empiricists? Or is it the case that true revelation occurs only within the Christian tradition and that God only discloses himself through his Word, written in Scripture, proclaimed in the Church, and incarnate in Christ?[4] This is precisely what Barth claims. He regards Scriptural revelation as unique. It is not just any sort of revelation that might be placed alongside other revelations. God reveals himself through himself and as the revealer he is identical with his act in revelation.[5] There is no attempt in the Bible to dissolve the unity of the self-revealing God, his revelation and his revealedness, into a uniformity. He is revealer, revelation, and revealed – it is this threefold mode of being, in unimpaired unity, which brings us face to face with the doctrine of the Trinity.[6] Barth's position is that it is the Trinitarian doctrine 'which fundamentally distinguishes the Christian doctrine of God as Christian – it is it, therefore, also, which marks off the

Christian concept of revelation as Christian, in face of all other possible concepts of God and concepts of revelation'.[7] When we ask the question who God is, the Bible answers in such a way as to point us to the three-in-oneness of God.[8]

The uniqueness of Scriptural revelation is further emphasized by Barth when he speaks of the biblical meaning of revelation as the self-unveiling of God who by his nature is inscrutable to man. The *Deus revelatus* is the *Deus absconditus*, 'the God to whom there is no way and no bridge, of whom we could not say or have to say one single word, has He not of His own initiative met us as *Deus revelatus*'.[9] He unveils himself to man who has no power to unveil him and the form he takes is the *humanitas Christi*. But the form does not take the place of God. It is not the form that reveals, but God in the form.[10] God the Father is God as Creator; God the Son is God as Reconciler; and God the Holy Spirit is God as Redeemer.[11]

If this is an accurate summary of what Barth claims concerning biblical revelation the question that arises is: by what independent criterion do we determine that revelation is unique or genuine in one instance and not in another? Or can it be that there is no independent criterion and that it is the revelation itself that enables us to state what is true and what is false? If so, what are we to make of the anti-Jansenist pronouncement of the Church *extra ecclesiam conceditur gratia*? If divine grace is believed to operate *extra ecclesiam*, then it operates in spheres other than the Christian tradition unless it is claimed that it operates only through the Church in its representative capacity. I shall have occasion to return to these questions later.

Another representative of neo-orthodoxy whose name is closely associated with that of Barth is Emil Brunner. Although his response to religious pluralism might also be classified as exclusivist it is of a more modified form. It shows marked differences from Barth's response and is characterized by a greater degree of openness to non-Christian religions. Differences between them emerge on the question of general revelation and *analogia entis*, Brunner affirming and Barth denying extra-biblical revelation and the retention of some form of *imago Dei* in man after the Fall. These differences have significant implication for the attitudes they adopt towards other religions.

In his assessment of revelation Brunner states that from the Christian standpoint it is absolute not relative. 'The God of the Bible is absolutely the God of revelation, because he is absolute and sovereign *Lord*, the unconditioned Subject.'[12] The Church lives by divine revelation and her task is to reflect on the story of God's saving acts. Revelation is neither a book nor a doctrine but God himself in his self-manifestation; it is the history of God's dealings with the human race. It follows that the history of revelation is the history of salvation and vice versa.[13] If revelation is a divine act, faith is the subjective act whereby the self-communication of God is received. The heart of faith is confidence or trust; it is an act of obedience to a gracious Lord.[14]

According to Brunner, God reveals himself in many different ways one of which is through his work in creation. There is, therefore, a general revelation or a revelation in creation. This is taught in scripture and finds support in the teaching of the Church fathers and the reformers. Barth admits that he goes beyond the teaching of the reformers but justifies his position on the grounds that the reformers failed to recognize the possiblity of an intellectual righteousness of works.[15] Brunner attributes Barth's opposition to the clear teaching of scripture and the consensus of opinion of Church theologians primarily to the fear of natural theology – the belief that it is possible to know God on purely rational grounds independent of, and apart from, revelation. Brunner, however, rejects that there is any connection between natural theology and biblical theology and insists that the reformers were well aware of this fact. He claims also that 'the question of revelation in creation and that of natural theology are two different questions'.[16] General revelation is as much the presupposition of particular, historical revelation as revelation in the Old Testament is the presupposition of revelation in the New Testament. Both have their own necessity and limitation. The primary significance of revelation in creation then is,

> that through it man as man is *person*, a responsible being, a being related to God, 'standing before' Him; and also that by this revelation man is responsible for his sin, and is therefore 'inexcusable'. This is why it is the presupposition of the saving revelation in Jesus Christ, although in itself it has no saving significance.[17]

Brunner makes it clear here that there can be no question of diminishing the glory of Christ or taking anything away from the doctrine of *sola gratia*. It is the same God who manifests himself through creation as speaks to us through the incarnate Word.[18]

The question that is now posed, given the exclusive claim of Christianity to revelation, is: how are we to understand the relation of the revelation in Christ to those claims to revelation put forward by other religions? Brunner's response is that Christian revelation is absolute, not relative. He rejects the relativistic conception of religion put forward by Schleiermacher, and later reformulated by Rudolf Otto, that there is an essence of religion, or a sense of the numinous, which underlies all religions and manifests itself in particular, historical forms. While the relativistic theory of religion would regard the essence of religion as fundamental, and distinguishing features as non-essential, for the Christian faith the exact opposite is true. It follows that 'Christian revelation and these "relative" theories of religion are mutually exclusive'.[19]

This is not to say that, for Brunner, traces of the idea of revelation do not occur in other religions. Even primitive religions show such traces but they can make no claim to be an authentic revelation comparable with the claim of the Christian revelation. Nor is the situation essentially different in the case of polytheistic religions, which differ only rationally or culturally from primitive religions. Neither can mystical religion lay claim to universally valid revelation; it simply points the way to revelation. Mystical experience might be called enlightenment, or illumination, as in the case of the Buddha, who, according to Brunner, never claimed to have received divine revelation. The distinction drawn between enlightenment, or illumination, and revelation here is an interesting one and might conceivably be based on what is considered to be the human source of the one as compared with the divine source of the other. Yet Brunner acknowledges that the enlightenment experience of the Buddha 'is understood as an event of supernatural character, as a mystical experience, through which he received the ultimate truth about the nature of the world, the reason for suffering, and the possibility of escaping from the latter.'[20] Despite its supernatural character, however, it differs from revelation because no self-revealing God is involved. Not even Amitabha Buddha, whose name is invoked by his followers to effect their salvation, can be considered to be God, the Creator and Lord. So

19

for Brunner there can be no justification for an enlightenment experience to be regarded as the universally valid revelation.

The case of the prophetic religions of Zoroastrianism, Islam, and Judaism is different: they *do* lay claim to be based on authentic revelation. Brunner acknowledges that they are impressive forms of religion and that there is a blood relationship between them and biblical religion, but he goes on to maintain that ultimately they are forms of rationalistic theism with moralistic overtones, yet lacking redemptive qualities. They offer no revelation of the holiness and mercy and the gracious mystery of God. What then are we to make of their claims to valid revelation? Brunner's response is that Mohammed never claimed to be a revelation of God in his own person; Judaism accepts the provisional character of its revelation and awaits the Messiah; and Zoroastrianism is simply the self-affirmation and self-confirmation of the natural moral consciousness. Only the Christian faith

> dares to maintain revelation in the strict, unconditional sense of the word, because it alone dares to assert, 'the Word became flesh'. Hence the radicalism of the claim to revelation is as unique as the content of the Christian message, the Atonement; indeed, in the last resort it is the same. For the self-communication of God is both complete revelation and complete reconciliation, the basis of faith *sola gratia*.[21]

What we can infer from this analysis of Brunner's position is that despite his greater openness to other religions and his acceptance of the concept of general revelation he is at one with Barth in insisting on the uniqueness of the revelation in Christ, the Word of God. For him the Christian revelation is not just one of the religions of the world; it is not 'one species of the genus "religion" ' except in so far as it considers itself to be 'the true religion in contrast to the other false religions'.[22] Yet he differs from Barth when he insists that the Christian interpretation of religion points to the fact that all religions presuppose the universal revelation of God in creation. Because God has never left himself without a witness among men it is possible to understand religions from the standpoint of his revelation in creation. This is the biblical doctrine of original revelation. But it is accompanied by the doctrine of original sin, the essence of which is apostasy and the tendency for man to become absorbed in himself. Because of his sin man's response to God's self-revelation is distorted and corrupted and he turns away from God to worship an idol, something of his own creation, whether in the form of an image or a depersonalized, abstract idea or principle.[23] The Christan attitude to other religions, therefore, takes the form of a dialectic. It is acknowledged that they constitute a response to God's self-disclosure, but it is also recognized that the reponse is often distorted and confused. The history of religions cannot in fact show a religious system that is fully spiritual, consisting of personal, revealed, and ethical elements, or a religion in which the truly human and truly divine are one. That is to be found 'only in that which is more than religion, in the divine revelation in Jesus Christ'.[24] Here Brunner echoes Barth, for Christ's revelation is both the fulfilment of, and judgement on, all religion; he is the truth that religions seek for in vain.

The question that arises naturally in relation to Brunner's position is why God should reveal himself through creation sufficiently to enable men to turn away from him to worship idols, but not sufficiently to effect their salvation. That is, why should general revelation be so ineffective in this respect as to require special revelation to supplement it? If it is the same God who reveals himself in creation as speaks to us through the incarnate Word, thereby making man responsible for his sin and inexcusable, why is it that his general revelation through creation should lack saving significance? This brings us back to the question of the uniqueness of the Christian revelation and the claim that it is absolute not relative.

Brunner's view finds further expression in the work of Hendrik Kraemer who was concerned with the Christian message in a non-Christian world. His book of that title, written in the year of the International Missionary Council held in Madras in 1938, challenged the prevailing liberal attitude to other religions as expressed in the American study of missions, edited by W. E. Hocking, published six years earlier and entitled *Rethinking Missions*. On the question of revelation Kraemer maintains that when properly defined it is apprehended only by faith. Christian revelation is the self-disclosure of God in Christ which is at once an act of salvation and judgement. It is the religion of the incarnation.[25] But what of the relation of Christian revelation to general revelation and natural theology? Are not nature and history sources of revelation also? Kraemer's response is that Christianity stands in a dialectical relation to the world, including non-Christian religions; it combines a 'yes' and a 'no'. It can say yes to the various efforts of man in 'higher' and 'lower' religions, and in philosophies and world views, to apprehend the totality of existence.[26] But while these efforts are often remarkable for their sublimity they are also pathetically ineffective, and wherever the religious consciousness of man is confused, distorted, and corrupted, as a result of his guilt and sin, the response of Christian revelation is no. Like Brunner, Kraemer insists on the uniqueness of the revelation in Christ.

> The Christian revelation places itself over against the many efforts to apprehend the totality of existence. It asserts itself as the record of God's self-disclosing and recreating revelation in Jesus Christ, as an apprehension of existence that revolves around the poles of divine judgement and divine salvation, giving the divine answer to this demonic and guilty disharmony of man and the world.[27]

But what of the problem of natural theology? Is it to be equated with revelation, or must a distinction be drawn between the two? Kraemer rejects Aquinas's attempt to embrace natural theology and Christian revelation in one harmonious system of thought on the assumption that the one is a preparation for the other. The uniqueness of Christian revelation, he claims, is sacrificed thereby to the demands of a harmonious system. On the other hand, he approves of Barth's stand against relativism and natural theology and his attempt to preserve the uniqueness of God's revelation in Christ, the exclusive nature of biblical truth, and the discontinuity of nature and grace. He does not think, however, that it is enough for Barth to say that God works outside the sphere of biblical revelation without discussing how he does so. 'Common sense and the reality of life revolt against this. Biblical realism requires us to wrestle with it, for the world is still the creation of God "who does not abandon the works of his hands".'[28]

Kraemer's view is that it is not permissible to equate general revelation or natural theology and the revelation in Christ as if they are of the same type and quality, or that they differ in degree rather than kind. Neither is it permissible to regard general revelation as a preparation for the fulness of revelation in Christ.[29]

General revelation can only mean that God reveals himself through nature and man's conscience because he chooses so to do. But general revelation is only truly understood in the light of the revelation in Christ. 'Here Biblical realism demonstrates again its deep and sound sense of reality, because it testifies that God's revelation in "general revelation" is just as well an object of faith as that in "special revelation".'[30]

The similarities between Kraemer and Brunner are evident and the questions raised in connection with Brunner's position apply equally to Kraemer, especially the question of the uniqueness of the Christian revelation and its claim to be absolute.

It is interesting to note that Kraemer's views on the uniqueness of the Christian revelation are echoed in his later work on the relation of Christianity to non-Christian religions.[31] He does not believe, however, that it is permissible to picture the relationship between Christianity and other religions in black and white terms. Neither does he believe that it is good enough to state simply that it all comes to the same thing in the end. Yet at the same time he is careful to distinguish between Christianity as a religion and Christ, whom he regards as the critic of all religions, and the criterion whereby all religions are to be judged. But how do we respond to the claim of religions other than Christianity to communicate the truth? Are not their beliefs and traditions impressive enough for us to admit that they have as much right as Christianity to claim to provide access to truth and goodness? Would it not be narrow-minded of us to say that the truth lies with Christianity alone? Kraemer admits that the question of the plurality of religions is problematic and that syncretism has its appeal. He cites Toynbee's plea for toleration, forbearance, and mutual respect as an illustration of this point of view, but concludes that the real nature of truth is distorted by this kind of approach.[32] Another approach is to maintain that all religions are different paths to the same goal and expressions of the same truth. Kraemer rejects this approach also on the grounds that it does not do justice to the facts, since profound differences exist between religions on the question of who, or what, is venerated as holy, or has unconditional authority. The same applies to the connotation of similar terms, such as salvation or revelation, which are used in different religions, but which turn out to be 'not merely radically different, but mutually irreconcilable'.[33] Equally unacceptable to Kraemer is the Hegelian classification of religions in order of priority according to their inherent truth or value.[34]

The ultimate criterion of truth for Kraemer is Jesus Christ, the revelation of God. The basis of Christianity is God's self-disclosure in Christ. Like Barth he insists that there is a radical distinction between religion and revelation and that as a historical phenomenon Christianity would have to be regarded as a religion alongside other religions and another example of man's quest for God. The revelation in Christ, however, is the result of God's initiative and that is why it is *the* criterion of truth. 'The absolutely distinctive and peculiar and unique element in Christianity is the *fact* of Christ'.[35] It differs from the fact of the Buddha or the fact of Mohammed in that Christ is the revelation in his own person; he is himself God's revelation. He does not communicate truths; he is the truth and as such he stands in judgement over all religions including Christianity. The similarities between this viewpoint and that put forward by Barth are evident especially on the question of the radical distinction between religion and revelation. For Kraemer, all religions, including to a great extent Christianity, are systems of self-justification and self-redemption and ultimately erroneous. Hence there is a discontinuity between revelation and religion. That which is disclosed in Christ is not capable of being discovered by the exercise of religious insight.[36] Kraemer's answer to the question of whether Christianity is an absolute religion, therefore, is an emphatic no. As a concrete, historical religion is on precisely the same footing as other religions and it makes no sense to say that it alone is true and the others false, '*there is no true religion*'.[37] Only the revelation of God in Christ is absolute and only there is the criterion of truth to be found.[38] The attitude of Christians to the adherents of other religions should be one of firmness and forbearance. It would be shortsighted, foolish, and unchristian to ignore them on the grounds that they are in error. Christians have much to learn from them, even about their own faith, and at the same time they have an obligation to witness to the revelation of God in Christ.

Kraemer's emphasis on the uniqueness of the revelation of God in Christ echoes the views of Barth and Brunner, and it also raises similar kinds of questions. But, as we have tried to show, it is clearly indicative of the neo-orthodox approach to religious plurality.

Chapter Three

THE RESPONSE OF RELATIVISM AND INCLUSIVISM: TROELTSCH, TOYNBEE

The absoluteness and exclusiveness of the neo-orthodox response to religious pluralism is in marked contrast to the relativity and inclusiveness of the attitudes adopted by Ernst Troeltsch and Arnold Toynbee, both of whom represent a more liberal theological approach. Troeltsch was very much aware of the importance of historical change and of the significance of the historical consciousness. He saw that all things were subject to historical development including cultural phenomena and religious and ethical ideas. The principle of development is so fundamental, he maintains, that we have to acknowledge the same 'development in religious, ethical, and philosophical ideas' and in 'the character of individuals and peoples', as we find 'in forms of government and economic conditions.'[1] It follows that we have to recognize also the transitory nature of all things, since historical consciousness seems to demand cultural relativity. But if all things are subject to historical development, including religious and ethical ideas, how does one reconcile 'historicism', or 'historical relativism' as it came to be called, with the absolute truth claims of Christianity?

This was the problem that Troeltsch sought to resolve and which he describes as the centre and starting point of his academic work.[2] He acknowledges the conflict that emerges from the acceptance of the significance of historical reflection on the one hand, and the attempt to determine standards of truth and value on the other. His humanistic and historical education, which involved him in historical investigation over a wide field, and the recognition of the infinite diversity and endless movement of human existence, was balanced by a personal need for 'a vital and effective religious position, which could alone furnish my life with a center of

25

reference for all practical questions, and could alone give meaning and purpose to reflection upon the things of this world.'[3] It was this personal need that led him to the study of theology and philosophy, but he soon discovered that his theological and historical interests conflicted with one another. That is, the critical attitude characteristic of his training as a historian contrasted significantly with the deep-seated desire of his religious conscious-ness to accept God's revelation and to obey his commands.

It is evident that, in Troeltsch's view, the comparative study of religion complemented historical reflection by virtue of the fact that it promoted the tendency to relativity and deepened the conflict between the historian's spirit of scepticism and the desire of religious consciousness for certainty. The attempts of theology to defend the truth of Christianity on the grounds that it is guaranteed by miracles, or that it is the most perfect expression of religion and, in the Hegelian sense, the culmination of the universal process of the unfolding of the divine Spirit, are rejected by Troeltsch. Apart from the critical attitude that might be adopted towards miracles, he maintains, one would have to face the fact that other religions, apart from Christianity, are able to lay claim to similar miracles. Again, on the question of Christianity as the most perfect expression of religion, it would have to be noted that a study of the history of religions does not indicate an upward trend culminating in Christianity. Furthermore, Christianity

> presents no historical uniformity, but displays a different
> character in every age, and is, besides, split up into many
> different denominations, hence it can in no wise be represented
> as the finally attained unity and explanation of all that has gone
> before, such as religious speculation seeks.[4]

Troeltsch makes it clear that Christianity, far from being the most perfect expression of religion, the culmination of the universal process of the unfolding spirit, or the goal of the forces of history, is nothing more than an individual manifestation of the Divine Life within history. The tendency of Divine Reason is to manifest itself in particular individual forms and Christianity is just one of these forms.[5] The question is, how does one go about defending the ultimate truth of Christianity? In his work *The Absolute Validity of Christianity* Troeltsch adopts the position that there is an element of truth in all religions coupled with many individual features. This truth can be recognized intuitively, and is the result of a profound personal experience and a personal conviction, which is later confirmed by its ability to solve life's problems. But in the case of Christianity its claim to universal validity is grounded in its faith in revelation which differs in kind and not just in degree from the belief in revelation to be found in other major world religions. While they tend to be nationalistic, as in the case of Judaism, Islam, and Zoroastrianism, or philosophical systems rather than religions, as in the case of Buddhism and Confucianism, Christianity eschews on principle all attempts to limit its appeal to particular races or nations, or to equate it with philosophical reflection. Its claim to universal validity is based on God's revelation of himself in men's hearts and lives; it is founded on the nature of God and man.[6]

The work that Troeltsch refers to as *The Absolute Validity of Christianity* was published under the title *Die Absolutheit des Christentums und die Religionsgeschichte* at the beginning of the century and was an expanded version of a lecture delivered in October, 1901. It appeared in English under the title *The Absoluteness of Christianity and the History of Religions* and is described by the author as an attempt to discuss, and if possible to overcome, the problems associated with reconciling philosophical reflection with the witness of the Christian community.[7] The implication for Christianity of the modern historical approach with its critical analysis of sources is recognized by Troeltsch. It made it impossible, as we have seen, to prove the normativeness of Christianity by having recourse to miracles since, irrespective of their critical attitude to miracles as such, historians could not be expected to accept Christian miracles and deny non-Christian miracles. Christianity could not be isolated from the rest of history, or on the basis of miracles be considered to embody the absolute norm of truth. The naïve certainty of Christian apologetics that the Church as a divinely ordained, supernatural institution, was founded miraculously, authenticated by the miracles of conversion and the sacraments, and sustained by the power of God, was untenable from the standpoint of the modern approach to history.[8]

The alternative theory that Christianity constitutes 'the actualization of the principle of religion, the absolute religion in antithesis to mediated and veiled expressions of this principle',[9] is, in Troeltsch's view, a form of the evolutionary apologetic. On this theory the principle or essence of religion, which is to be found in all religions, finds its most perfect expression in Christianity. That being the case Christianity must be considered to be the norm of religious truth, since the essence of religion is at one with the principle of Christianity. The similarity between the traditional apologetic of the Church and the evolutionary apologetic of idealists like Schleiermacher is evident. According to Troeltsch, both are concerned with the absolutenness of Christianity, yet, as he points out, the difference between the two, namely, 'supernatural revelation' on the one hand, and the 'absolute fulfilment of the essence of religion' on the other, cannot be ignored.[10]

Troeltsch's response to the evolutionary theory concerning Christianity is that it is impossible to construct such a theory on historical grounds. The modern idea of history, in his view, 'knows no concept of a universal principle that embodies a law governing the successive generation of individual historical realities.'[11] It follows that it knows of no law determining the essence of religion or the norm of truth. He views with a sense of disquiet those theological works which treat the principle or essence of religion as some kind of power underlying individual religions, and Christianity as the absolute realization of that principle. Such works subordinate historical investigation in the modern sense to the concept of a universal principle, which in turn is elevated to the position of a norm.

Our knowledge of the history of religions, Troeltsch maintains, leads us to believe that it is not possible to speak of the essence of religion in such a way as to include both a normative principle and a graduated manifestation of that principle. Furthermore, the modern study of history gives no indication that there is a progressive development from lower to higher forms of religious life culminating in Christianity. The higher religions are not related to one another in this way; rather, they stand in a parallel relationship to one another.[12] It is not possible on historical grounds to regard Christianity as the absolute religion. Like other religions it is a concrete, historical religion, which is conditioned by the historical situation in which it finds itself. At no time is it the absolute religion or 'the changeless, exhaustive, and unconditioned realization of that which is conceived as the universal principle of religion.'[13] From the standpoint of the modern approach to history, therefore, the attempt to present Christianity as the absolute religion and the most perfect expression of the essence or principle of religion, is untenable.[14]

The modern approach to history, however, does not prevent the Christian from recognizing the personal, redemptive religion of Christianity as the highest truth for himself based on his personal conviction. It is 'absolute', therefore, according to Troeltsch, in the sense that for him it is 'the highest value discernible in history', 'the way that leads to perfect truth' and 'the purest and most forceful revelation of the higher world'.[15] It is on the basis of this belief that the Christian is able to maintain the Christian religion to be normative not only for himself but for the whole of mankind. That is not to say that other religions, with their power to deliver men from grief, guilt, and anxiety, are not in their turn revelations of God, but 'Christianity remains the great revelation of God to men'.[16] It is the work of Jesus and derives its strength from the guarantee of God's grace in his person. The prophets of other religions may also reveal the power of God, but it is revealed in Christianity more profoundly than anywhere else. It is possible that Jesus may be surpassed one day but not probable, for 'Christianity is the pinnacle of all religious development thus far and the basis and presupposition for every distinct and meaningful development in man's religious life in the future.'[17]

These conclusions concerning the status of Christianity are modified in Troeltsch's later writings. He stresses, for example, that the concept of the individual manifestations of the Divine Life within history is not so easily reconciled with the Christian claim to supreme, universal validity. Christianity is above all a particular, historical religion determined to a great extent by the different circumstances of life. It assumes different forms depending on the intellectual and social conditions in which it finds itself; that is, it is culturally determined. Furthermore, the claims of non-Christian religions to absolute validity is as genuine as the Christian claim, and religions like Buddhism and Hinduism (or Brahmanism, as Troeltsch calls it), appeal to the conviction and devotion of their followers in the same way as Christianity does to its adherents. As the particular, historical character of Christianity comes more to the fore, so the concept of supreme or absolute validity retreats more into the background. This is not to say that Christianity lacks truth, or ceases to be a manifestation of the Divine Life. The profound inner experience and personal conviction of Christians guarantees its validity, but only its validity for them.

> It is God's countenance as revealed to us; it is the way in which, being what we are, we receive, and react to, the revelation of God. It is binding upon us, and it brings us deliverance. It is final and unconditional for us, because we have nothing else, and because in what we have we can recognize the accents of the divine voice.[18]

Other religious groups belonging to different cultures may experience manifestations of the Divine Life which are equally valid for them, but this applies only to those nations that have attained a high level of civilized life. It is interesting to note here that Troeltsch excludes the less developed races from these manifestations, including what he calls 'the simple animism of heathen tribes'.[19] Why he should do so is not clear, neither is it clear by what criterion he classifies animistic tribes as heathen. It could be argued that in order to understand the customs and traditions of other people, the onus is on us to extend and broaden our understanding of their way of life rather than insist on seeing everything in terms of our ready-made distinction between what is scientific and unscientific, or civilized and uncivilized. I shall have occasion to return to this point again; suffice it to say at this stage that the importance Troeltsch attaches to the concept of civilized life is further evidenced by his statement that in order to determine the relative value of religions we have to take into consideration the civilizations of which they form a part.

The practical implications of this modified view put forward by Troeltsch relate to attitudes adopted to missionary activity and the spread of Christianity. It influences, for example, the attitude one adopts to the concept of missions and the question of conversion, which is related in turn to the concept of the absolute validity of Christianity. Troeltsch points out that Christianity must stand in a different relationship to the other major religions of the world from its relationship to the heathen tribes. The former may benefit from contact with Christianity, and their development in depth and purity may be promoted thereby. However, no conversion from one to the other can be contemplated, rather the concern must be for mutual understanding. The latter on the other hand have a claim on missionaries to provide them with a substitute for the way of life that may be destroyed by their contact with civilization. On the question of the development of Christianity on the other hand, Troeltsch notes that it is closely related to the development of European civilization. While it possesses a religious consciousness which is less subject to change than the more temporal aspects of civilization, it is, nevertheless, involved in the literary and philosophical speculation characteristic of civilized life. This makes its development unpredictable for it is always capable of assuming new forms.[20]

The emphasis placed by Troeltsch on cultural relativism and the linking of particular religions to specific cultures, and on epistemological relativism, which speaks of Christianity as the truth for Christians but not necessarily for all people, is further clarified by his insistence that all religions have a common goal in the Beyond or the Unknown, and a common ground in the Divine Spirit. Historical religions, however, although they move in the direction of ultimate unity and objective truth, manifest individual differences which are likely to remain. Hence, according to Troeltsch,

> so far as the eye can penetrate into the future, it would seem
> probable that the great revelations to the various civilizations
> will remain distinct . . . and that the question of their several
> relative values will never be capable of objective determination,
> since every proof thereof will presuppose the special
> characteristics of the civilization in which it arises'.[21]

Mutual understanding occurs when each religion seeks to realize its own potential, yet, at the same time, is open to the influence of others in their quest for truth, for the 'earthly experience of the Divine Life is not One, but Many'.[22]

Troeltsch's tendency in his earlier work to extend the normativeness of Christianity to the whole of mankind is modified significantly, as we have seen, in his later writings. His mature position is clearly that religions are culturally determined, that Christianity is influenced by its intellectual and social milieu, and that it is normative for Christians alone and not necessarily for all mankind. It is for this reason that he is regarded as epitomizing the relativistic approach to religious plurality.

The response to religious pluralism of Arnold Toynbee is a further example of the liberal theological approach which was in marked contrast to the exclusivist approach of neo-orthodoxy. His major contribution to scholarship is *The Study of History*, a work in twelve volumes in which he examines the rise and fall of twenty-six civilizations. He assigns religion a significant place in the history of civilizations which, he maintains, serve a religious purpose. All the higher religions offer man the means of salvation, but they do so in different ways, and Toynbee's view is that they should concentrate on what unites them, or what they have in common, rather than on what divides them and distinguishes them from one another. His aim and purpose is to promote harmony among world religions and to eliminate dissension.

His views are epitomized in the Hewett Lectures delivered at the Andover Newton Theological School, the Episcopal Theological School, Cambridge, and Union Theological Seminary, New York. He describes the lectures as a discussion of the attitudes of Christians towards other world religions. He admits that he does not expect to see, nor does he advocate, the establishment of a single religion from the merging of existing historical religions. But he raises the question whether they should not stand together to proclaim that which is common to them all, namely, that man is not the measure of all things, nor the highest spiritual presence in the world.[23]

His first lecture examines the criteria that might be used for a comparison of religions. He looks at the possibility of regarding beliefs and practices, or the conduct of adherents, as criteria for comparison and concludes that they are not acceptable. What is acceptable, he maintains, is what one might call the spirit of religion, that is, the attitude of higher religions towards man, evil, and suffering. Similarities and differences would emerge, but at least these criteria would bring out the stronger and weaker points of the different world religions.[24]

He discusses the characteristics of the contemporary world in his second lecture, particularly the expansion of modern Western civilization and the growth of technology. As he points out, this civilization is basically post-Christian and secular, and has produced a revival of totalitarianism or 'of man-worship in the form of a worship of collective human power'.[25] If one asks what the relation of Christianity is to the Western civilization that has unified the contemporary world, Toynbee's reply, which is to be found in his third lecture, is that among its many incidental activities it has functioned as a midwife for the birth of Western civilization. But he also predicts that Christianity will continue to be a living spiritual force in the world long after Western civilization has ceased to be, and that the role of the latter in history will prove to be a minor one compared to the role of the former.[26]

It is the relation of Christianity to non-Christian faiths, however, that is the main concern of his final lecture, and he is at pains to point out that the higher religions ought to make new approaches to one another, and seek common ground, in the face of a revival of the worship of what Thomas Hobbes referred to as the 'Leviathan', or that collective human power which is armed with technology.[27] What action then should be taken by Christians in order to meet followers of other faiths on common ground? Toynbee suggests that, as a first step, Christians should purge Christianity of its Western, Graeco-Roman accessories which tend to make it a tribal religion of Western civilization. His second suggestion is that Christians should relinquish the traditional belief that Christianity is unique, and with it the exclusive and intolerant approach to other religions. He claims that it is possible to believe that the fundamental truths of Christianity are a revelation from God without insisting that they constitute the sole and unique revelation. That God revealed himself to Christians is not in doubt, but given his nature it seems unlikely that he would not have revealed himself to other people as well.

> And it would seem unlikely that He would not have given His revelation in different degrees, according to the difference in the nature of individual souls and in the nature of the local tradition of civilization. I should say that this view is a corollary of the Christian view of God as being love.[28]

He acknowledges that it is far more difficult to purge Christianity of exclusiveness than it is to remove its Western accretions, yet he considers it essential that this should be done. The main reason he offers for this is that exclusiveness manifests pride and self-centredness, which is incompatible with the concept of a self-sacrificing God, and that arrogance and intolerance had led to the rejection of Christianity in the past and could well do so again in the future.[29]

The Christian approach to other religions, in Toynbee's view, ought to include in some measure the acknowledgement that they reveal what is right and true; that they come from God; and that they shed spiritual light derived from the same source as that of Christianity. The revelation given to mankind through other religions may differ in degree from the revelation given through Christianity, but it does not differ in kind. God is the God of all mankind. The more the world continues to be unified, the greater will be our acknowledgement of other cultures. Gandhi, for example, commanded the allegiance of Hindus because he was nurtured in their way of life, but this did not prevent him from acknowledging the influence of Christianity. Toynbee foresees the possibility of people making a free choice of the religion they wish to follow as the world grows closer together and in this respect he is not so very far removed from the Mahatma he admires.[30]

His recognition of the unification process at work in the world does not, however, lead him to maintain that a syncretistic religion ought to be constructed out of the various elements of the different religions of the world. These would be artificial constructions and would not capture the imagination or allegiance of men. Neither does he anticipate that historical religions will coalesce to form one religion, though he does express the hope that they might become more open-ended and open-hearted towards one another, while at the same time holding fast to their own truths and ideals and retaining their own historical identities. Like Gandhi, he believes that respect and reverence for other faiths would enable men to understand and practise their own religion better. He approves of the practice of proclaiming Christian truths and ideals to non-Christians, in deeds as well as words, but advocates also receptiveness to the truths and ideals of other faiths in order to avoid the sin of arrogance and intolerance.[31]

On the question of the essential elements of Christianity Toynbee lists three. First, the concept of a God who so loves men that he sacrifices himself for their salvation; second, the conviction that men should follow the example set by God in the incarnation and crucifixion of Christ; and third, that this conviction should be a matter not just of theory but of practice. But he makes the point that these essential elements are not exclusively Christian and that they have parallels in other religions. This leads him to maintain that it is possible to have 'conviction without fanaticism', and 'belief and action, without arrogance or self-centredness or pride', since the mystery of man's encounter with God is not approached by one road only.[32]

Toynbee's position is sufficiently clear to warrant the claim that it is in marked contrast to the exclusivist approach to religious plurality and that it merits being classified as inclusivist. But his position is inclusivist, as we have shown, not in the sense that he advocates the creation of a syncretistic religion, nor the coalescence of different historical religions to form a single, universal religion, but rather in the sense that it is recognized that revelation differs only in degree and not in kind. The spiritual light that shines through other religions is derived from the same source as that of Christianity, namely, the God of love who reveals himself to all men in accordance with their ability to receive his revelation. This makes the exclusivist concept of the once-and-for-allness, or uniqueness, of the revelation of God in Christ untenable, and one of the main characteristics of Toynbee's inclusivist stance is his belief that Christianity needs to be purged of this form of exclusivism.

Chapter Four

THE ESSENTIALIST RESPONSE: SCHLEIERMACHER, HOCKING, OTTO, JUNG

Another theological response to religious pluralism is that which is related to the quest for the essence of religion. As we have already indicated, Hegel may well have been one of the first thinkers to regard religion as a self-subsisting essence, or a transcendent entity, underlying all historical manifestations. But Schleiermacher also conceives of religion as pre-existing individual, historical manifestations. For him, the concept of religion as a transcendental entity is the necessary prerequisite for the existence of historical religions, which may be regarded as concrete expressions of the primordial form, the immediate religious consciousness, 'the sense and taste for the infinite'.[1] Not that particular religions are superfluous; the plurality of religions is in fact necessary for the full and complete manifestation of the transcendental unity of religion, because each religion embodies something of the essence of religion. Historical religions can be considered more or less true, therefore, to the degree that they succeed in expressing the essence, or primordial form, of religion.[2] The multiplicity of historical or positive religions, according to Schleiermacher, is the direct result of the work of the spirit, and although they may contain much that is corrupt and degenerate, they also possess, to a greater or lesser degree, something of the true nature of religion. It is possible for religions to be arranged in an ascending scale of importance linked to the evolutionary development of man's religious consciousness, from so-called primitive forms of nature and image worship, through polytheism, to monotheism, of which Islam, Judaism, and Christianity are considered to be the main representatives. Of the positive religions, however, Christianity, in Schleiermacher's view, is the most sublime, glorious, and penetrating, the most perfect and highly developed form of religion. For him, it is the fulfilment of the religious development of mankind, the culmination of a progressive, evolutionary development from a lower to a higher form of religious experience. Yet he acknowledges that the compatability of all things human is such that the possibility of more beautiful and impressive forms of religion cannot be dismissed or ruled out.[3]

Schleiermacher is often referred to as the theologian of romanticism, the school that owed its origin to Goethe and was a protest against the tyranny of rationalism and abstract thought. His speeches on religion addressed to its cultured despisers have been referred to as the religious programme of romanticism. They incorporate the sentiments of the romantic school especially in respect of its views on nature and history, individuality and religion. What he endeavoured to do was to show his cultured, literary friends that religion is not simply a theological system, or a set of theories, doctrines, principles, or ideas, or even analyses of the nature of an incomprehensible being, but something that has to do with the soul of man. Religion is far removed from all that is systematic, for systems merely house the dead letter and not the spirit of religion. Religion ought not to be confused with the external, doctrinal shell. To discover what religion is one must turn from what is usually called religion and look within at the pious soul. The kernel is the exalted mind, the 'soul dissolved in the immediate feeling of the Infinite and the Eternal'. This is the primordial form of religion.[4]

For Schleiermacher, the starting point of religion is man; it has a human ground. It originates in the soul's response and surrender to the Universe, the One, the Whole, the Godhead, the Infinite. True religion is the 'sense and taste for the Infinite'.[5] Naturally this definition has given rise to accusations of psychological subjectivism against Schleiermacher, especially in view of his rejection of rationalism. But it would be a mistake to assume that his stress on feeling, or sense and taste, implies simply an emotional response without any intellectual content. While he would concede that conceptual thought cannot comprehend the fundamental unity, the One, the Infinite, the Absolute Spirit, grounding the ideal and the real, thought and being, or mind and nature, it is the case, nevertheless, that feeling, or intuitive awareness, or immediate self-consciousness, provides the basis for understanding the fundamental ground of knowledge. Feeling, for Schleiermacher, is not simply an emotion, or a sense of rapture; 'sense and taste for the Infinite' cannot be classified as subjectivism. It is an a priori cognitive experience; it is the means by which the ground of knowledge is understood.

It is this injunction to recognize and understand that religion has a human ground, and that it originates in the pious soul's response and surrender to the Universe, that leads Schleiermacher to insist that it cannot be equated with its outward finite forms, nor confused with science or morality. What is known of the nature of things is not religion. 'Religion cannot and will not originate in the pure impulse to know'.[6] Neither is religion to be equated with ethics, though the excellence of ethical systems would be acknowledged and it would be recognized that one cannot be pious without being moral. Religion is, in fact, the natural counterpart to science and morality: an indispensible third. It is the feeling that all that influences us is One; that everything is part of the Whole.[7]

But can we talk about religion without mentioning God and immortality? According to Schleiermacher, both are presupposed in what he has to say about religion. The usual conception of God is of a being outside and behind the world, but this is only one way of expressing the idea of God and it is certainly not the beginning and end of religion. It may be necessary for some to think of God in this way because of their need for consolation and succour, but such a God can be believed in without piety. The true nature of religion is immediate consciousness of the Deity as we find him in ourselves and the world. Not all who reject anthropomorphism in relation to God ought to be classified as despisers of religion, for God can be conceived of as the highest and only unity, in whom we see the world as the Whole, the Universe.[8] Similarly, the usual conception of immortality is of a goal outside or beyond time; something that is yet to come after this temporal life. But the true goal of the religious life is the immortality that we have now within time. 'In the midst of finitude to be one with the Infinite, and in every moment to be eternal, is the immortality of religion'.[9]

In Schleiermacher's view the primordial essence of religion finds expression in the sorry form of earthly religions. Each positive religion is a distinct, though impure, form of religion in its essence. The multiplicity of earthly religions is necessary, as we have seen, for the complete manifestation of religion.[10] While it is true to say that positive religions are full of much that is not religion, and distinguished by elements that they should endeavour to eliminate, such as empty customs, abstract ideas, and claims to absolute truth, nevertheless they are forms of religion, and embody much of the true nature of religion.[11] Each historical religion is a distinct form of religion and a way of revealing it, for religion is the sum total of man's relation to God apprehended in different ways. There is no universal religion natural to all. Individuals differ in their receptiveness to different religious feelings and experiences.[12] Antipathy to religious multiplicity should be avoided. Every man is entitled to develop his own religion, though most men will choose an existing form of religion if it corresponds to his own feelings, and it is none the less individual or personal on that account.[13] Christianity is one of the positive, historical religions and of a high order, yet it ought not to be equated simply with the words of Jesus, or his moral teaching. It expresses man's longing for the Infinite and brings to perfection the indwelling of the Divine Being in finite nature. It brings the finite closer to the infinite through the work of mediation, which participates in both the human and the divine.[14] Not that this means, in Schleiermacher's view, that we are entitled to regard Christianity as the only true religion. Nothing it seems would be more irreligious than to deny multiplicity and demand uniformity. Different types of religions are always possible, given different degrees of apprehension and receptivity on the part of man, and it has to be acknowledged that new religious developments are always capable of taking place alongside Christianity.[15]

In his work *The Christian Faith* Schleiermacher develops further the notion of the sense and taste for the infinite when he defines religion as the feeling of absolute dependence, or the consciousness of being absolutely dependent, which he equates with being in relation with God.[16] He also elaborates on his view of the distinctiveness of the Christian faith. The point has been made by Cantwell Smith that the usual translation of the title of this work, *Der Chistliche Glaube*, which includes the definite article, is inappropriate, and that even *Christian Faith*, which has been used from time to time, may have to give way to something like 'faith in its Christian form'. In which case the book is about Christian piety 'and *other forms* of faith'.[17] It has to be acknowledged that there does seem to be sufficient evidence in Schleiermacher's writings to support the claim that Christian piety is just one form of piety, or religion, among many, and that there is a case for stating, as Cantwell Smith does, that 'we have no option but to reflect on faith generically'.[18] But what is it in the relation of mankind to the infinite that is distinctive in the Christian form of faith and that justifies considering it to be the most perfect and highly developed form of religion? And how is this to be reconciled with the claim that other religions, or forms of faith, are not to be considered false since they too contain an element of truth and an awareness of the infinite?

Schleiermacher seeks to answer these questions by noting that different religious traditions embody different forms of faith and indicate different stages of development. The superiority of the Christian faith is not in doubt, but that is not to say that other forms of faith are false or erroneous. If subordinate forms of faith contained nothing but error, how would it be possible for men to pass from them to the higher truth of Christianity?[19] The monotheistic, teleological form of faith exemplified in Christianity is, according to Schleiermacher, 'the most perfect of the most highly developed forms of religion',[20] and distinguished from other faiths 'by the fact that in it everything is related to the redemption accomplished by Jesus of Nazareth'.[21] As Redeemer, Christ is the manifestation of divine revelation in history, yet in Schleiermacher's view, he is neither absolutely supernatural nor absolutely supra-rational. Since Christ was a man, then it follows that human nature has the potential of taking up the divine into itself. Therefore, no absolute distinction can be drawn between the supra-rational quality of the Redeemer and common human reason, for reason is at one with the divine spirit.[22] The feeling of absolute dependence is actually presupposed in every religious self-consciousness; it represents the finitude of our being and as such is a universal element of life.[23]

But to return to the question originally posed. What is it in the relation of mankind to the infinite that is distinctive in the Christian faith? The answer seems to lie in the person of Christ who, by virtue of his identity with human nature and the potency of his God-consciousness, which is synonymous with the existence of God in him, is the Redeemer of mankind.[24] His redemptive activity is effected through the communication of his sinless perfection. This consists in imparting to man his consciousness of fellowship with God; and we have fellowship with God when we have living fellowship with Christ.[25] The Christian form of faith is distinctive, therefore, because it is the expression of the life of the ideal man in whom the most perfect form of God-consciousness has been manifested.[26] The rational self-consciousness and God-consciousness that belonged to human nature originally cannot really be called the existence of God in us. This brings us to the second question concerning the truth of other forms of faith. For Schleiermacher, God-consciousness prior to the advent of the Redeemer was not pure and tended to be dominated by sensuous self-consciousness. This was the case with polytheism, and even Jewish monotheism, both of which were affected by materialistic conceptions.[27] But just as the unconscious forces of nature and non-rational life can become a revelation of God to us, so too imperfect God-consciousness can become the existence of God in us. Yet it is

> only through Him (Christ) that human God-consciousness becomes an existence of God in human nature, and only through the rational nature that the totality of finite powers can become an existence of God in the world, [so] that in truth He alone mediates all existence of God in the world and all revelation of God through the world, in so far as He bears within Himself the whole new creation which contains and develops the potency of the God-consciousness.'[28]

This seems to imply that, for Schleiermacher, while the revelation of God is possible through other forms of faith, it requires the potency of the God-consciousness of Christ as the new creation, or to use Schleiermacher's terminology, the Second Adam, for it to be made effective. This is what makes the Christian form of faith distinctive, the most perfect and highly developed form of religion, and the fulfilment of the religious development of mankind. Even so, for Schleiermacher, Christianity cannot be regarded as the universal religion, or the only genuine type of religion. The Deity can be contemplated and worshipped in a variety of ways and 'As nothing is more irreligious than to demand general uniformity in mankind, so nothing is more unchristian than to seek uniformity in religion.'[29] So despite his emphasis on the distinctiveness of Christianity as the most highly developed form of religion, Schleiermacher insists that it cannot be considered to be the only genuine form of it, and that the existence of a variety of historical religions is necessary in order to reveal the essence of religion. The essentialist response to religious plurality, therefore, as found in Schleiermacher, is positive, and makes the claim that without religious diversity and multiplicity the transcendental unity, or primordial form, of religion is not fully manifested. That is, for the essentialist, religious pluralism is absolutely essential for the manifestation of the essence of religion.

The essentialist approach to religious pluralism is to be found also in the reconception theory of W. E. Hocking. His Hibbert Lectures, delivered in 1936 and published in 1940, deal with what he refers to as the 'rightful future relationship of the great religions, what attitudes they should hold to one another, and with what justification we might look forward to the prevalence of one of them as a world faith'.[30] He regards missionary activity as an attempt to make a particular religion universal, but the primary interest of those concerned with world culture and world citizenship, he maintains, is to escape from such an emphasis on particularity and to discover in religions that which is already universal.[31] He defines religion as the will to live well, a passion for righteousness, the rejection of the illusion of privacy, the redemption of solitude, and as that which relieves man of self-concern.[32] Religion, he maintains, must be universal because it is a 'hopeful passion', a 'universal human craving', which is directed towards a universal object, 'an absolute, in the sense that it holds good for all men in all places at all times'.[33] The way to human unity, in his view, is to be actively concerned with an absolute goal or end.

But, according to Hocking, if religion has to be universal it has also to be particular. Since man's moral destiny is identified with the moral destiny of the group within which he lives and acts, his religion, of necessity, will have a regional character and history; that is, it will be a particular religion.[34] We find the most significant and conspicuous manifestations of particularity in the ritual observances of different religions since ritual is the visual expression of communal feeling. So the universality of religion is limited by its particularity, and the dilemma of religion is that the universal can never fully sanction the particular, since that which is actual is tainted by the very fact of its actuality. Where there is insistence on the importance of the historical character of a particular religion, there is also a proportionate resistance to any attempt to make a particular religion the world faith.[35]

Hocking has no desire to reduce the number of particular religions in the world any more than he desires the conversion of all religions to one so-called true religion. He notes that the Chinese consider it natural to be both Confucianists and Buddhist, and he concludes from this that if particular functions are successfully performed by one religion, and universal and transcendental functions by another, then two religions are likely to be better than one.[36] His examination of the traits of oriental religions leads him to conclude that they are not easily refuted, or classified simply in terms of an evolutionary or dialectic order.[37] The metaphysical thinking characteristic of these religions is a powerful factor in bringing about rational agreement among men and in effecting the assimilation of religions, though not, as we have seen, in successfully creating a single, so-called true, religion.[38] With the emergence of a world culture, however, the possibility of the creation of a world faith, which would combine universality and particularity, is greater than it would otherwise have been, and Hocking addresses this question with the development of his theory of reconception.

He regards the religious intuition of the soul as the common ground of all religions and the primary factor binding them together in the struggle against secularism. Religious experience, he claims, is characterized by the twin movements of broadening and deepening. In these days, the broadening of experience occurs when different faiths encounter one another and discover, through mutual contact, aspects of truth not previously envisaged. This in turn leads to the deepening process, which is the search within a particular religion for a better understanding of its own essence in the light of the new aspects of truth that have emerged. The deepening process demands that the particular religions concerned be reconceived in order that previously unnoticed characteristics within them are brought to light.

At the present time, the demand of the deepening process is for a better understanding of the essence that underlies all forms of religious life. It is no easy task to discover what this essence is, but it can be discerned by a process of induction; that is, by coming to understand, or recognizing the reason, why it is that a group of experiences belong together. The broadening process assists in the task of discerning the essence of religion by pointing to what is similar in different faiths. Hocking speaks of this broadening as the process of synthesis and the deepening one as the process of reconception. Synthesis is the natural preparation for reconception and the deepening process of reconception makes the process of synthesis less a separate movement and more a spontaneous aspect of life.

The quest for the essence of religion which is part of the deepening process of reconception is progressive and unending. As self-understanding within a particular religion deepens and a better understanding of its own essence emerges, so it is enabled to grasp the essence of all religions. The process of reconception, therefore, conserves rather than destroys what is valuable in other traditions. It does so by anticipating what the beliefs of adherents of other traditions mean to them, and by helping them to express the meaning of their faiths; for example, in the case of ancestor worship in China, its essence is the importance of the family bond for the community, and the doctrine of the void in Buddhism might be interpreted in terms of the ineffable of mystical experience. The guiding principle is that the ideas of others are allowed to develop in their own way or 'given the benefit of their direction'. It may be appropriate to point out at this stage that however altruistic the process of reconception may be in seeking to help adherents of other faiths to express the meaning of their faith, it may well prove to be misguided. To interpret the Buddhist doctrine of the void, for example, in terms of the ineffability of mystical experience, may well be regarded as a typical attempt to fit this doctrine into a preconceived Western pattern of thought. A similar attempt was made by Indian scholars when they sought to subsume Buddhism in Advaita Vedanta. This would hardly be in accord with the principle laid down that the ideas of others be 'given the benefit of their direction'.

Hocking sees the process of reconception, however, as a method that might lead to a world faith. It is not that particular religions would be replaced by a universal religion, or that one particular religion would radically displace all other religions, but that the mutual contact of religions would produce deeper self-understanding. This in turn would lead men to question which religion diagnoses correctly the problems of human life; most effectively liberates from greed, hatred, and other afflictions; and proves most fertile in sustaining the artistic life and conferring the eternal peace of God. This process of reconception, he maintains, stands in need of an institution in which study and learning, meditation and contemplation, worship and artisic activity, might prevail. A chain of such institutions might be established to reconceive religion through world culture, and similarly to reconceive world culture through religion. Hocking refers to the ashram founded by Rabindranath Tagore at Santiniketan, where adherents of different faiths engage in creative, artistic work, meditation and worship, and social activity, as analogous to the kind of institution he has in mind.[39] Clearly, what Hocking envisages is a better understanding of the essence of one's own religion from an acquaintance with the insights of other religions, and since he conceives the essence of all religions to be the same, he sees the reconception approach, which conserves what is best in each religious tradition, as leading eventually to the establishment of a world faith.

The essentialist way of reconception, through mutual contact and learning among the religions of the world, differs from the way of radical displacement associated with the exclusivist approach of Barth and Kraemer, and also from the way of synthesis associated with the more liberal, theological approach, although Hocking acknowledges that the latter might be regarded as a first stage on the way of reconception. The essentialist way of reconception, however, has more in common with the approach of Otto, with his concept of the numinous, and with the approach of Schleiermacher. The latter as we have seen, conceived of religion as pre-existing individual, historical manifestation, and considered particular religions to be grounded in the a priori transcendental unity of religion, the primordial form, as expressed in 'the sense and taste for the infinite'.[40] The similarity between Hocking and Schleiermacher on the question of the essence of religion is evident, although the latter, as we have seen, views that essence as progressively manifested in the religious development of mankind and most perfectly fulfilled and embodied in Christianity. Hocking's views, however, reflect his particular philosophy of personal idealism which, it is claimed, seeks a middle way between absolute and pluralistic idealism.[41]

The essentialist approach is to be found also in the work of Rudolf

Otto, who exercised a profound influence with his philosophically significant book *The Idea of the Holy*, in which he attempts to provide a phenomenological analysis of the structure of religious consciousness. He openly acknowledges his admiration for Schleiermacher, whom, he maintains, rediscovered religion. In his examination of the concept of the holy, which, as the sub-title of his book indicates, is an enquiry into the non-rational factor in the idea of the divine, and which he considers to be the heart of religion, he succeeds in making a significant contribution to the essentialist response to religious pluralism.

The term 'holy', for Otto, is the key word of all religions and in his analysis of the concept he distinguishes between what he calls rational and non-rational elements. One of the rational elements is that of moral goodness, but it would be a mistake to assume that such rational elements fully explain the meaning of the holy since 'religion is not exclusively contained and exhaustively comprised in any series of "rational" assertions'.[42] The core of the concept of the holy lies in its non-rational element, for which Otto coins the term 'numinous', a derivation of 'numen'. Rational concepts such as moral goodness, completeness, and necessity may be predicated of the numen, but in itself it is indefinable, since as a mental state it is 'perfectly *sui generis* and irreducible to any other'.[43] Rational elements are clearly essential to the understanding of religion, but they do not epitomize, or fully explain, the meaning of religion. The non-rational element of religion, as Otto explains, is to be found in the numinous, the nature of which is revealed in the way it grips and stirs the mind through feelings or affective states. Numinous feelings differ from feelings of beauty or of the sublime; they are characterized by what might be called the sense of creatureliness, which is accompanied by the feeling of awe or dread on the one hand, and the feeling of fascination and attraction on the other. These feelings are evoked, for example, by the atmosphere of temples and churches; by the solemnity of rites and liturgies; and by the presence of an inexpressible mystery. They give one the clear impression of being confronted with what Otto calls the *mysterium tremendum*. In his analysis of this phrase he refers to the wholly other, the unapproachable nature of the mystery with which one is confronted, and which elicits the feeling of fear or dread and the sense of awe. It is this feeling which is the basic impulse and starting point of man's religious development. In primitive man it takes the form of demonic dread, and in more recent times manifests itself in the feeling of horror or terror on hearing ghost stories, for example, or the feeling of awe which causes the limbs to tremble, the flesh to creep, and the hair to bristle. Numinous feeling may differ from demonic dread, but the sense of awe remains even at the highest level of religious development.[44]

A further element of the *mysterium tremendum* is that of power and majesty. It is the awe-inspiring, overpowering majesty of the numinous that induces the sense of creatureliness which is at the root of religious humility. Otto compares this with Schleiermacher's 'feeling of absolute dependence', but whereas Schleiermacher means by this phrase man's sense of createdness, Otto has in mind man's consciousness of creatureliness in the presence of the awesomeness and overpowering majesty of the numinous. This consciousness of creatureliness, he claims, is one of the characteristic aspects of that type of mysticism which seeks identification of the self with transcendental reality.[45]

A third element of the *mysterium tremendum* is energy, which assumes symbolic form in such terms as vitality, passion, will, force, and wrath. It elicits accusations of anthropomorphism from the more philosophically inclined, but, for Otto, it represents non-rational aspects of the divine nature nevertheless, and protects religion from being over-rationalized. It is preserved, like the sense of creatureliness, in certain forms of mysticism.[46]

Otto makes a further point, namely, that the *mysterium tremendum* is also *fascinans*. It not only repels by means of feelings of awe or dread in the presence of the overpowering majesty of the numinous, but it also fascinates and attracts, evoking feeling of wonder, reverence, and love.

> The qualitative *content* of the numinous experience, to which 'the mysterious' stands as *form*, is in one of its aspects the element of daunting 'awefulness' and 'majesty'. . .but it is clear that it has at the same time another aspect, in which it shows itself as something uniquely attractive and *fascinating*.[47]

We have already noted that, for Otto, numinous feelings differ from natural feelings, such as the feeling of beauty or the sublime. Numinous feelings, though analogous to natural feelings, are in fact unique. They do not evolve from natural feelings; they emerge from the sense of the numinous, the nature of which is revealed through affective states. Numinous feelings are, therefore, cognitive. They may be cognitive in the sense that they refer to an objective, numinous reality, the encounter with which, through numinous experiences, gives rise to the concept of the numinous. In that case the concept of the numinous is a posteriori in the sense that it emerges from the experience of an objective, numinous reality. On the other hand, numinous feelings may be cognitive in the sense that they produce both the concept of the numinous and at the same time disclose the objective, numinous reality to which the concept applies. In which case the concept of the numinous is a priori. On either interpretation, Otto is claiming that numinous feelings reveal an objective, numinous reality which he terms numen.[48] It is this non-rational element of the numinous which, for him, lies at the heart of the idea of the holy and which is the essence of all religions.[49] It is the common ground of religious consciousness; it 'issues from the deepest foundation of cognitive apprehension that the soul possesses'.[50]

Although Otto is primarily concerned with providing a phenomenological analysis of the structure of religious consciousness, by his isolation of the non-rational element of the numinous as the core of the concept of the holy, he is at the same time indicating that which constitutes the common ground, or essence, of all religions. This has important implications for the study of religions, and his influence on those who have been concerned with religious plurality has been significant. Tillich's concept of religion, for example, together with his dynamic-typological approach to the study of religions, owes much to this phenomenological analysis. It is Otto's belief that the concept of the holy is the common ground or essence of religion, however, that marks him out as a significant representative of the essentialist approach to religious plurality.

A further significant contribution to the common ground or essentialist approach to the study of religion is to be found in the work of Carl Gustav Jung, who, contrary to Freud, adopts a positive attitude to religion and expresses his belief that it is a natural element in the life of man and necessary for his psychological health. He claims:

Among all my patients in the second half of life – that is to say, over thirty-five – there has not been one whose problem in the last resort was not that of finding a religious outlook on life. It is safe to say that every one of them fell ill because he had lost that which the living religions of every age have given to their followers, and none of them has been really healed who did not regain his religious outlook.[51]

While both Freud and Jung have a naturalistic view of religion, the difference between them is that the latter does not accept Freud's atheistic viewpoint, preferring instead to uphold a form of agnosticism that leaves open the question of the nature of ultimate reality and to adopt a more positive appraisal of the value of religion.

Jung claims that man has always needed the help that religion can give, which is what Freudian psychoanalysis overlooks when it brings the shadow side of man's psyche to the conscious level and then leaves man to cope with it as best he can. Opening up the unconscious is like unleashing hordes of barbarians, in Jung's view, which is why man has developed religious practices to arm himself against this threat, and why religions prove beneficial in healing psychic illnesses. This is especially true of the two great religions of Christianity and Buddhism. The psychotherapist, Jung maintains, has often been forced to act as a priest and to deal with problems that more properly belong to the domain of the theologian. It is his belief that the psychotherapist cannot ignore these problems, and he proceeds in the hope that forces of healing will emerge from the depths of the psyche that originally produced the destructive powers.

The human psyche is referred to by Jung as 'one of the darkest and most mysterious regions of our experience',[52] and the depths of the psyche is the region he calls the collective unconscious, which contains archetypes capable of assuming independent existence and serving as spiritual guides in man's life. The religious man would say that his guidance came from God, but with most of his patients Jung avoids this kind of reference, speaking instead of the psyche awakening to spontaneous life. The archetypes effect the transformation of destructive powers into healing forces and bring about the end of man's illness. It is as if, from the depths of the psyche, something emerges to confront man and begin the process of healing. Jung claims that the spontaneous activity of archetypes, whether or not understood by the conscious mind, are manifestations of the spirit, which help the sufferer to resolve the conflicts that exist within himself and bring about the integration of his personality. The psychotherapist, he maintains, would welcome the understanding of the Church in this healing task for he recognizes that the manifestations of the spirit are wonderfully varied and capable of being constantly renewed in the history of mankind.[53]

The point that has to be made here is that Jung advances his theory of the collective unconscious to account for the recurrence of the same symbols in dreams, myths, works of art, and religions. It is a hypothesis he designs to explain why certain archetypal images constantly recur in literature, art, Eastern religious writings, and in the dreams of his patients. Yet it has to be acknowledged that he seems to regard the unconscious not just as an explanatory hypothesis, but as something that actually exists, an established fact. He is at pains to point out, however, that the fact of the unconscious cannot be presented in such a way that would satisfy the criteria of science or logic.[54]

The collective unconscious, in which archetypes or primordial images exists, is, for Jung, the deposit of the collective experience of mankind through the ages. These primordial images 'are the most ancient and the most universal "thought-forms" of humanity. They are as much feelings as thoughts; indeed, they lead their own independent life.'[55] They are 'capable of endless development and differentiation' and the archetype of the God-image points to a correspondence between the soul and God. As the eye corresponds to the sun so the soul corresponds to God, which is the primary reason that it is 'psychologically unthinkable for God to be simply the "wholly other", for a "wholly other" could never be one of the soul's deepest and closest intimacies – which is precisely what God is.'[56] The man who fails to realize that religion, the *mysterium magnum* is rooted in the human psyche and not just an outward form of faith does not know what religion is.[57] This is not a question of deifying the soul, but simply recognizing that the soul has a religious function, and that there is a correspondence between it and the outward image. 'Accordingly when I say as a psychologist that God is an archetype, I mean by that the "type" in the psyche.'[58] What psychological research does is to point to the correspondence between archetypes and religious ideas, whether those ideas, for example, relating to the First Cause, take the form of God, Purusha, Atman, or Tao. It opens men's eyes to the meaning of religious dogmas, and provides them with the opportunity to understand other primordial images or archetypes that religious teachings have to offer. While religions would stress the form of the First Cause, referring to it as God, Atman, etc., psychology would emphasize the archetype or primordial image, which in its indefiniteness could not be fully expressed by any definite religious form. Jung's name for this corresponding archetype is the 'self', which is sufficiently indefinite to allow a variety of determinate forms to symbolize it, and both the Christ-symbol and the Buddha-symbol are highly developed and differentiated symbols of the 'self'.[59] This then is the reason for Jung's positive attitude towards religion; it is for him a form of the archetypal 'self', a manifestation of the spirit, and it is efficacious as a therapy for the soul. People belong to the Catholic Church, for instance, because they feel at home there, and primitive religion is clearly more suitable for primitive people than any form of Christianity, which would be foreign and alien to them.[60]

Jung distinguishes between religion and creeds which he considers to be codified forms of religious experience and not to be regarded as embodiments of the eternal truth.[61] Yet creeds have an important function in society in the sense that immediate experience is replaced by symbols, invested, as in the case of Christianity, with the authority of the Church.[62] The psychologist, however, has to be concerned with the original experience, which dogmas, rituals, and creeds symbolize. Were he to be bound to the creeds he would not be free to interpret the spontaneous activity of the archetypes of the unconscious which 'can be shown empirically to be the equivalents of religious dogmas'.[63] What is true of the creeds applies also to religions and, as we have seen, Jung considers it 'inconceivable that there could be any definite figure capable of expressing archetypal indefiniteness'.[64] He concludes that God may have manifested himself in many forms and many languages, and far from one manifestation being true and the others false, all manifestations are true.

But what of the claim to uniqueness made for the revelation of God in Christ? The Christ-symbol, says Jung, is of great importance and a most highly developed symbol of the 'self'. But the same applies to the Buddha symbol, and experience of the archetype of the 'self' can lead one man to the truth of Christ and another to the truth of the Buddha.[65] It follows that no religion can lay claim to finality or absoluteness. While the archetype of the 'self' might take the form of Christ for some, it could take the form of Purusha, Atman, Hiranyagarbha, or the Buddha for others.[66] So from his psychological starting point, with the archetype of the 'self' corresponding to religious ideas relating to the First Cause, Jung arrives at an approach to the different religious traditions of the world which is not in any way dissimilar to that of other essentialist responses to religious pluralism.

Chapter Five

THE CATHOLIC RESPONSE: KUNG, SCHLETTE, RAHNER

Another form of the theological response to religious pluralism is that which regards Christianity as embodying the fulness of God's grace and revelation and is related to the concept of salvation history. It finds expression in the writings of Catholic theologians of whom Kung, Schlette, and Rahner might be considered notable representatives. According to this assessment of religious plurality, all non-Christian religions have a place in God's plan of salvation. They undoubtedly manifest the grace of God, but their role in the pattern of salvation is preparatory. The plenitude of grace and the fulness of salvation is to be found only within the Christian tradition. It is presupposed, presumably, that the concept of salvation must mean the same thing in different religious traditions, though why this should be so is not at all clear. It is also presupposed that the concept of God as Lord of history, which has a precise meaning within the Christian tradition, must apply in the same way, or have the same meaning, in other religious traditions. The approach is sometimes referred to as representing a liberal Catholic attitude to non-Christian religions. It is a view that favours dialogue, and one that rests on a wider vision or concept of God than that which would confine his revelation to a single religious tradition.

Hans Kung expresses this view very well and is a notable exponent of the liberal Catholic approach. He was one of the people appointed as official theologian of the Second Vatican Council by Pope John XXIII and one of the few Catholics to recognize the importance of dialogue with non-Christian religions. His acquaintance with the tolerance shown by people like Radhakrishnan and Gandhi towards the great faiths of the world, and as exemplified in their writings,[1] led him to query whether their vision of God was not greater and more exalted than those traditionalists who would confine God to one religious tradition. The classic testimony of Catholicism, proclaimed by Pope Boniface VIII, is still to be found embodied in Denzinger's *Enchiridion* which states that:

> We are required by faith to believe and hold that there is one holy Catholic and apostolic Church; we firmly believe it and unreservedly profess it; outside it there is neither salvation nor remisssion of sins. . . . Further, we declare, say, define and proclaim that to submit to the Roman Pontiff, is, for every human creature, an utter necessity of salvation.[2]

Kung questions whether the doctrine *extra ecclesiam nulla salus est* could possibly be maintained with honesty today when one considers the countless millions of people, both past and present, who have lived, and are living, outside Christianity and the Catholic Church. Again, how is it possible to maintain such a doctrine when one considers the countless millions who are going to live outside the bounds of Catholicism in the future? He makes the point that Christian mission as previously practised in the age of colonialism and the Western domination of the world is no longer viable, and, as far as the people of Asia are concerned, 'over and done with'. In a period which has seen the renaissance of world religions it makes little sense to speak of 'no salvation outside the Church'. Neither is it possible to resort to 'dialectical theology', and, by means of an a priori concept of religion, interpret non-Christian religions as indications of human autonomy in the quest for God. This is Kung's explicit rejection of the neo-orthodox response to religious plurality. It is as wrong for Christians, he maintains, to present neo-orthodoxy as self-evident as it is for them to compensate for their ignorance of world religions by making arrogant judgements about other religions. The fact remains that after two thousand years of missionary endeavour there is no significant change in the pluralistic religious situation.[3]

According to Kung, the Christian theological resolution of the problem of religious pluralism lies in assessing positively the significance of non-Christian religions in God's plan of salvation. It involves a move from an ecclesiocentric view to a theocentric view, and the setting aside of the misleading axiom *extra ecclesiam nulla salus est.* That men can be saved outside the Catholic Church is not in doubt, and the Second Vatican Council explicitly recognizes the fact that 'if some men do not know the Father of our Lord Jesus Christ, yet acknowledge the Creator, or seek the unknown God in shadows and images, then God himself is not far from such men, since he gives life and inspiration to all (cf. Acts 17, 25–8), and the Saviour wills that all men should be saved (cf. 1 Tim. 2.4)'.[4] But what are the consequences for non-Christian religions of the Christian adopting a theocentric rather than an ecclesiocentric approach? It means, says Kung, that the God of the Bible is acknowledged as the God of all men, and that he is capable of being known by all men. This knowledge of God must not be regarded as typifying 'natural' religion, however, or the activity of 'natural theology', but rather as a human response to the revelation of God's grace in creation. That is, the theocentric approach affirms that God revealed himself to man prior to his revelation in Christ. As the Second Vatican Council's declaration on the relation of the Church to non-Christian religions affirms: 'His manifestations of goodness, His saving design extend to all men, until that time when the elect will be united in the Holy City, the city ablaze with the glory of God, where the nations will walk in His light.'[5] The *extra ecclesiam* doctrine is not in accord with the theocentric approach, since God's plan of salvation embraces all men, and makes it possible for us to give a positive account of the significance of non-Christian religions.

What form, we may ask, does this positive response to non-Christian religions have to take? According to Kung, it does not follow automatically from the acceptance of the theocentric approach that we have to affirm the concept of an absolute, mystical experience common to all religious traditions, of which all religious forms are relative expressions. It may be true to say that there is common ground, or that there are parallels to be drawn, between religious traditions, which makes spiritual communion between different religions possible, but that is a far cry from claiming that the underlying mystical experience alone has ultimate validity, and that religious traditions are simply relative forms of that experience. Such an affirmation is as much a matter of faith as the claim that God has revealed himself fully and completely in Christ alone. The impersonal approach of mysticism is no less dogmatic than the personal approach of Christianity, or

Judaism, or Islam. But given the dogmatic presuppositions of the Christian tradition, how are the non-Christian religious traditions to be regarded? It can be maintained from the dogmatic standpoint, says Kung, that (a) they are in error; (b) they proclaim the truth of God although in error when they acknowledge man's need of salvation, recognize God's grace, and listen to the voice of their prophets; (c) there are ordinary ways of salvation for non-Christian humanity as distinct from the extraordinary way of salvation provided by the Church. That is, non-Christian religions exemplify universal salvation history as distinct from special salvation history. Both types of salvation history are the result of the grace of God, for it is his will that all men should be saved. But every man is intended to find his salvation within his own religious tradition and his own historical milieu, for he is essentially a social being, and his religion always finds expression in a social form. God sanctions religions as social structures and it is man's duty to seek God within the religion that is made available to him. These religions, however, have only a 'relative validity' [6] and a 'relative providential right to existence'.[7] They may prove to be the way of salvation by the grace of God, but they need not necessarily be so. Outside the Church there is only the ordinary way of salvation; within the Church lies the extraordinary way of salvation.[8]

It is interesting to note at this point, that despite Kung's emphasis on the theocentric as opposed to the ecclesiocentric approach in the positive assessment of the significance of non-Christian religions, he returns to what appears to be an ecclesiocentric approach when it comes to distinguishing between ordinary and extraordinary ways of salvation. He does not deny, it is true, that salvation is possible *extra ecclesiam*, yet it is ordinary as opposed to extraordinary salvation, and it is those who reside within the Church, those who believe in Christ and confess him, who are the vanguard of humanity and the visible sign of the fulfilment of all things. Real salvation and true communion between man and God is only possible through the Gospel of Christ. It is in Christ that God has acted uniquely for all men. Religions are structures which contain both the light of revelation and the darkness of human error and failure. They are pre-Christian rather than non-Christian, and stand in need of the Gospel to liberate the truth.

On the basis of this analysis Kung claims that he is propounding neither the domination of one religion nor the syncretism of all religions, but rather a Christian ministry to human beings in other religious traditions in the spirit of dialogue. The truth of other religions is acknowledged, but the Christian faith is not relativized. It may eschew exclusiveness, but it still lays claim to uniqueness. The Church is still the work of God, and continues to issue a challenge to the adherents of non-Christian religions to unite with her in witnessing to Christ. That is, the Church extends an invitation to Christians *de jure* to become Christians *de facto*.[9]

Kung seems to be referring to this ecclesiocentric approach when, in a later work, he refers to what he calls the new interpretation of the *extra ecclesiam* doctrine put forward by some Catholic theologians. The Church means for them all men of good will who are from the beginning 'anonymous' Christians. 'The formula, "no salvation outside the Church", is then as true as ever, because all in fact are in the Church from the very beginning: not as formal but as "anonymous" Christians or – as we ought logically to say – "anonymous Roman Catholics".'[10] That he finds this version of the new interpretation less than acceptable is evident from his somewhat scathing remark about all men of good will being elegantly swept into the back door of the Catholic Church across the 'paper-thin bridge of a theological fabrication'.[11] No sincere, self-respecting Muslim or Jew, he claims, would take kindly to being referred to as an anonymous Christian, any more than Christians would take kindly to being called anonymous Buddhists. It has to be admitted, therefore, that to stretch the meaning of the concepts of Church and salvation in this way is an unsatisfactory answer to the challenge of non-Christian religions. Better to admit honestly that there is salvation outside the Church and then examine the truth claims of Christianity in the light of this admission.[12] The question of salvation in non-Christian religions does not make the question of truth irrelevant for Christians. 'However much truth they (other religions) exhibit in certain respects, which Christians must affirm, they do not offer the truth for Christians.'[13] Whether or not this marks an advance on Kung's previous position, according to which non-Christians are invited to unite with the Church in witnessing to Christ, it is clear that the question of the uniqueness of Christianity and the claim of its followers to possess the fulness of the truth remain.

Schlette expresses a similar point of view to that of Kung as we have seen from his reference to non-Christian religions as having 'a relative providential right to existence'.[14] He too regards salvation history, or the history of redemption, as the basis for his theological interpretation of non-Christian religions. He readily admits that the openmindedness required for the theological study of the history of religions is not always present. But while the apologetic approach is unacceptable, so also is the syncretistic approach which undermines the uniqueness of the Christian faith.[15] If we enquire what is meant by salvation, or redemptive history, we are told that it is the sum of all that God effects in the history of mankind for the redemption of humanity, yet it is co-extensive with secular history and, therefore, does not take place outside world history, or the historical features and social structures of the human situation.[16] It has to do with the salvation of mankind in accordance with God's plan. It is possible to discern such salvation, or redemptive history, operating generally in the non-Christian religious traditions.

> If general sacred history can and must be held to be positively willed by God, then non-Christian religions also have to be considered to be willed and sanctioned by God . . . and even if it must be admitted that on this road errors and obscuration were not lacking, it is not possible on principle to contest the legitimacy of religions, which has its grounds in the theology of general sacred history.[17]

But general sacred history, which provides the ground for the ordinary ways of salvation of non-Christian religions, is fulfilled by special sacred history, which is the occasion of an extraordinary way of salvation. This is the full manifestation of divine glory in Christ, who is the eschatological event indicative of special sacred history. The extraordinary way of salvation is definitive, and its relation to ordinary ways of salvation is the relation between what is perfect to what is less perfect.

> Yet if special sacred history exists, the primary significance of which is the epiphany and glorification of God, it must not be lost sight of that the non-Christian religions, like all that is human and as yet incapable of experiencing and recognizing the full self-communication and unreservedly manifest character of grace, are imperfect.[18]

The implication of this distinction is that, for Schlette, the recognition of the significance of non-Christian religions does not detract in any way from the distinctiveness of the Christian faith. For it is the absolute revelation of God's saving power in Christ, through the Church, that makes it possible for us to raise the question of the role of ordinary ways of salvation in non-Christian religions in the first place. That is, it is in the light of special sacred history that ordinary ways of salvation can be recognized for what they are and verified as coming from God. But for Christian theology the unity of sacred history is of faith, and 'the salvation which is also attainable by the ordinary ways of general sacred history is the redemption brought by Jesus Christ and as such is the salvation mediated by the Church'.[19] This is Schlette's way of insisting on the uniqueness of the Christian faith. What occurred prior to the revelation of God in Christ was not insignificant, or unimportant, and demands respect, since it provided a relationship between man and God decisive for salvation, but it was less than perfect. Hence a transition is required from religions to faith so that dialectic fulfilment might take place. That is, faith is not simply the continuation of what went before nor its destruction, but true fulfilment whereby imperfection is perfected. This is Schlette's way of justifying conversion – or transition, as he calls it, since religions as such cannot be converted – from non-Christian religions to the Christian faith, without giving the impression of being too exclusivist. He actually disapproves of conversion apologetics while at the same time recognizing the need of a move from religions to faith. He characterizes the apologetic approach of both dialectical theology, and the fulfilment theology of Aristotelean-Thomism, for example, as too simplistic and extreme to be satisfactory. It was far too frivolous, in his view, to classify the positive elements of non-Christian religions as isolated phenomena, or illusory, fragmentary, incomplete, and subjective, since they too bore witness to genuine religious sensitivity and contained remarkable testimonies to the experience of the holy. Yet he is prepared to acknowledge the positive contribution of dialectical theology in stressing the uniqueness of the revelation in Christ, and in claiming that the Christian faith is not simply an extension of natural theology, but something attainable only through God's grace. His insistence on the need for a transition from religions to faith, in fact, does not place him in a theological position so far removed from that of dialectical theology. Nor does his concept of dialectic fulfilment differ in kind, or to any significant degree, from the fulfilment theology of Aristotelean-Thomism which he decries as simplistic and extreme.[20]

Schlette recognizes that his theological interpretation of the significance of non-Christian religions does not detract in any way from his insistence on the uniqueness of Christianity, or from the claim that might be made that it embodies the fullness of truth. It is precisely because of this that he is able to examine the significance of non-Christian religions in the way that he does. Whether he faces the particular problem of the truth claims of non-Christian religions is another question. The same point could be made of Kung's views. It might be argued that a move towards a more open, or a more radical, approach to non-Christian religions is barely perceptible in either case. It is true that it represents a giant step forward from the view that would classify all 'religions' as unbelief, but does it differ substantially from that view in respect of the claim of the Christian faith to possess absolute truth? What can be said, however, is that Schlette acknowledges the relevance of a theology of non-Christian religions, and that he considers toleration to be grounded in the nature of God himself.[21]

Schlette and Kung echo views that are to be found in the writings of Karl Rahner, for whom non-Christian religions are social structures representing a tangible expression of God's redemptive will that is universal. He recognizes religious pluralism to be one of the major facts of human existence with which the Church has to come to terms.[22] He sees it as a threat to Christianity because, as he says, no other religion lays claim so absolutely to be the one and only revelation of God. The days of 'other' religions, which hardly merited serious consideration, he claims, are over. No longer can the west isolate itself, or consider itself to be the centre of history, for 'everybody is the next-door neighbour and spiritual neighbour of every one else in the world.'[23] So-called alien religions are part of our existential situation, which makes the problem of religious pluralism an urgent one. His attempt to respond to the problem and to offer a Catholic, dogmatic interpretation of non-Christian religions takes the form of four theses which might be summarized as follows:

(i) Christianity understands itself to be the absolute religion which is intended for all men. It is the true and lawful religion which binds man to God. Although it has a prehistory going back to the beginning of the history of humanity, it also has a beginning in history and 'has not always been *the* way of salvation for men – at least not in its historically tangible ecclesio-sociological constitution and in the reflex fruition of God's saving activity in, and in view of, Christ.'[24] The question is whether or not the demand of Christianity in its historical, tangible form takes place at the same time for all men or not. Rahner leaves this an open question, but insists that wherever in practice Christianity is presented to man, it is the only valid religion and the necessary means of his salvation.

(ii)   Non-Christian religions are the means of a natural knowledge of God, but they are also the source of supernatural grace freely given to man because of Christ. This is so until such time as the Christian religion becomes part of the historical situation of an individual. Whether this refers to Pentecost, or whether it means a different time for different people, is left an open question. But if it is the Catholic view that there is no salvation apart from Christ, and that God has willed the salvation of all men, then these two propositions can be reconciled, says Rahner, only by stating that all men are the recipients of God's supernatural grace. Therefore, it can be maintained that grace has been offered outside the Church and that non-Christian religions 'must not be regarded as illegitimate from the start, but must be seen as quite capable of having a positive significance'.[25] If man is always and everywhere capable of being a *homo religiousus*, then he is capable of being so in the context of the concrete religion in which he and others lived in his time. For God's saving purpose for man is intended to reach him through the particular religion of his actual, historical situation.[26]

(iii)   As recipients of God's supernatural grace, members of non-Christian religions must be regarded as anonymous Christians. If a pagan, using the term as a theological concept and non-pejoratively, has experienced the grace of God, then he has already received divine revelation irrespective of whether he has been the target of missionary activity. Again, if through *fides implicita* he has experienced Christ's salvation, since there is no other, then it follows that he has to be regarded as an anonymous Christian. The proclamation of the Gospel, however, produces a higher development of Christianity and the explicit awareness and acknowledgment of what was previously dimly realized; the anonymous Christian becomes a fully committed Christian who has a clearer grasp of the nature of Christianity and a greater chance of salvation.[27]

(iv)   If non-Christian religions constitute an anonymous form of Christianity, then the Church cannot regard itself as having an exclusive claim to salvation. Rather it must be regarded as the vanguard, or the explicit expression, of that hidden reality which is present in non-Christian religions. It may be considered presumptuous on the part of Christians to regard non-Christians as anonymous Christians, or non-Christian religions as anonymous Christianity,[28] but, says Rahner, the Christian cannot be expected to renounce his presumption because, in Paul's words, he proclaims what men do not know and yet worship (Acts 17.23).[29]

Rahner's theological, or Catholic dogmatic, interpretation of non-Christian religions does not detract in any way from his insistence on the uniqueness of Christianity. Non-Christian religions may be an anonymous form of Christianity, but the proclamation of the Gospel is still required for the implicit to be made explicit, or the hidden reality to be made manifest. The fullness of truth, and the completeness of revelation, is only possible through the revelation of God in Christ. To use Kung's terminology, non-Christian religions provide ordinary ways of salvation, while the extraordinary way of salvation is possible only through the Gospel of Christ, and those who believe in him are the vanguard of humanity and the visible sign of the fulfilment of all things. What we have said hitherto concerning the views of Kung and Schlette can be repeated in respect of Rahner's position. The particular problem of the truth claims of non-Christian religions remains unresolved, and the move towards a more open and radical approach to religious pluralism continues to be barely perceptible. Nevertheless, it is a step forward from the position that would ignore their existence as irrelevant. At least it is fully recognized that the plurality of religions is a fact that cannot be ignored and one which has to be taken into account by those who would offer a Christian understanding of human existence.[30]

Chapter Six

THE DYNAMIC-TYPOLOGICAL APPROACH: TILLICH

A significant reponse to religious pluralism is to be found in the writings of Paul Tillich. He is careful to remind us of the basic considerations, or prerequisites, that a Christian theologian must have in mind in order that he might take seriously the task of constructing a Christian theology of religions. In the first instance he would have to reject the usual distinction drawn between *vera religio* and *religiones falsae*, or the belief that we have revelation and faith on the one hand, and religion on the other. In other words, he would have to reject the exclusivist approach to religions, which, as we have seen, was characteristic of the neo-orthodox response to religious pluralism, and accept instead the view that revelatory experiences are universal and received by man in the historical context of specific human situations, which by their very nature tend to distort revelation.[1] The similarity between this attitude and the views expressed on this point by the Catholic theologians we have examined is clear, but before proceeding to develop Tillich's position it might be appropriate to look at the views he expresses in his earlier writings. He makes the claim, for example, that there may be a central event in religious history which would make possible a particular theology of universal significance. He refers to this central event as the *kairos*, or the significant event, of the appearance of Jesus as the Christ. There are other *kairoi* in the history of religions, or momentous events of great religious significance, but the relation of the *kairos* to the *kairoi* is 'the relation of the criterion to that which stands under the criterion and the relation of the source of power to that which is nourished by the source of power'.[2] The *kairos* is unique, and *kairoi* are rare symbolic moments, but together they determine the dynamics of

63

religious history. If we ask Tillich on what grounds he is able to justify the claim that the appearance of Jesus as the Christ is 'a moment in history for which everything before and after is both a preparation and a reception', his reply is that it is precisely an expression of the daring courage of the Christian faith which without the risk of error would not be faith.[3] Yet even the possibility of error seems to be removed when he confidently asserts, that 'even for an empirical and relativistic approach' there is 'no other event of which this could be asserted', and then goes on to claim that the appearance of Jesus as the Christ 'is not only the centre of the history of the manifestation of the Kingdom of God; it is also the only event in which the historical dimension is fully and universally affirmed'.[4] The implication of this statement is that history can only be fully understood from the point where history reveals its meaning, namely, in the appearance of Jesus as the Christ as the centre of history. This is Tillich's Christological interpretation of history, which was enthusiastically welcomed by D. M. Baillie, who compared it to the time scheme worked out by Barth.[5]

Tillich's claim that the *kairoi* of the history of religions are a preparation for the *kairos* of the appearance of Jesus as the Christ, which is normative, is again not dissimilar to the views of the Catholic theologians we have examined; for them special sacred history and the extraordinary way of salvation in Christ is definitive and final, as opposed to general sacred history and ordinary ways of salvation which are preparatory. It may well be that the daring courage of the Christan faith applies in each case, but when Tillich seeks to give a fiducial guarantee for the significance of the historical event of Jesus as the Christ, is he not guilty of a misuse of religious language? He distinguishes, for example, between the element of probability in our knowledge of the historical Jesus and the certainty we have concerning the factualness of the Christ event, by which he means the factualness of the personal life which lies behind the biblical picture of Jesus as the Christ. It is difficult to understand why the personal life that lies behind the biblical picture of Jesus as the Christ should not be subject to the same kind of historical investigation as the personal life of the historical Jesus. It would appear that Tillich applies one criterion of historical truth to the question of the historical Jesus, and another criterion of historical truth to the question of the factual element of the Christ event. He accepts the necessity for radical historical investigation into the life of the historical Jesus, yet he would guarantee, on the basis of faith, the historical existence of the personal life in which the New Being appeared, and which finds expression in the biblical picture of Jesus as the Christ. Such a fiducial guarantee gives the distinct impression of seeking to provide the Christian faith with a sheltered zone, free from the harsh winds of historical investigation and criticism. It is, I suggest, an example of the misuse of religious language. To say that the experience of the reality of the New Being guarantees the factual element of the biblical picture of Jesus as the Christ, is tantamount to making the truth of a religious experience the norm, or criterion, for establishing the truth of a historical fact. The question that arises is why Tillich should endeavour to make the historical basis of the Christian faith immune from the normal investigatory processes of historical research. One possible explanation is that his interpretation of the meaning of history rests squarely on a Christological foundation. The appearance of Jesus as the Christ is, for him, the event which both affirms the historical dimension and reveals its meaning. It follows that the historical basis of Christianity ought not to be made dependent on the vagaries and uncertainties of historical research, and the only solution to the problem is for faith to guarantee its own historical foundation. This, however, makes a religious judgement normative in a historical context, which lends force to the accusation that Tillich is guilty of a misuse of religious language. It is important to note, however, that he is not guilty of adopting the Barthian approach, which would consider the *kairoi* of history to be examples of man's futile attempts to reach God by his own efforts, and of having no meaning or significance in themselves.[6]

It is difficult to see, given the logic of the argument, how Tillich can possibly deny to other religious traditions a similar interpretation of history based on what *they* consider to be the *kairos* of revelation, and which for them would be an expression of the daring courage of *their* faith. It is not altogether clear either how he can defend the claim he makes for Jesus as the Christ on purely empirical grounds. The appearance of Jesus as the Christ may be decisive for Christians, and the event of the cross may well be *their* criterion of truth, but what is to prevent a different *kairos* being decisive for the adherents of another religious tradition, or a different momentous, symbolic event being the criterion of truth for them? The question is, how do we distinguish between *kairoi*, and on what grounds do we determine which *kairos* is the universally true criterion?

When he comes to study the history of religions Tillich propounds what he calls a dynamic-typological approach to religious experience, which he later applies to the encounter of Buddhism and Christianity. This approach shows the influence of Rudolf Otto's work on *The Idea of the Holy*, with its analysis of the holy as *mysterium tremendum et fascinans*, its stress on the experience of the holy as the sacramental basis of all religions, and its emphasis on the mystical movement as an expression of dissatisfaction with any particularization of the holy.[7] According to Tillich, there are three main elements in man's experience of the holy, namely, the sacramental, the mystical, and the prophetic, and his evaluation of mysticism as an irreducible element in every religion is basically in agreement with the views expressed by Otto.[8] These three elements in religious experience, when harmoniously united, produce what Tillich calls the Religion of the Concrete Spirit, that is, the kind of religious experience all religions strive for, and which occurs only in fragmentary form in particular, historical religions. His stress on the fragmentary nature of the Religion of the Concrete Spirit, or the ideal type of religious experience, stems from his acknowledgement that in referring to religious types, or religious typology, he is really talking about abstractions. In fact, he refuses to conceive of a universally valid religion of the spirit existing in the abstract, as it were, unrelated to, or divorced from, particular, religious formulatons. He insists rather, that the Religion of the Concrete Spirit, or the ideal type of religious experience, which harmonizes the dynamic-typological elements of the holy, can be found only in the depths of particular, religious traditions. It is the *telos*, or inner aim, of all religions, he maintains, to become the Religion of the Concrete Spirit, and it manifests itself in the struggle against those demonic and secular forces which seek to oppose and resist the sacramental basis of religion. So, for Tillich, the future of theology lies in an intensive period of interpenetration between theological studies and religious studies, and he sees the possibility of some kind of theological structure emerging in the future from the very fact that there are fragmentary manifestations of theonomy, or the Religion of the Concrete Spirit, in the depths of particular religions.[9]

Tillich is not entirely happy with his dynamic-typological approach to the history of religions and expresses his dissatisfaction with it.[10] I share his dissatisfaction, but not for the same reasons. He recognizes that to talk of religious types is to talk of abstractions, since, as he says, types are logical ideals and do not exist in time and space. Hence his insistence on dynamics and dialectics, and the importance of recognizing the benefits to be derived from the interaction of the different type-determining elements which might predominate in different religions.[11] His recognition of the abstract nature of religious types, however, only leads him to acknowledge that there can be no ideal Religion of the Concrete Spirit, or a universally valid religion of the spirit (in which the sacramental, mystical and prophetic elements in the experience of the holy are harmonized) existing in the abstract and unrelated to particular religious traditions.[12] It does not prevent him, however, from conceiving of an ideal form of religious experience in the first place, of which particular religious experiences are but partial and fragmentary manifestations. His position in this respect is not far removed from that of Schleiermacher, for whom the essence of religion, the primordial form, pre-exists historical manifestations as an a priori condition, and is comprehended in and through the language and traditions of particular, historical religions. The question that might be asked is whether it makes sense to speak of the sacramental, mystical, and prophetic elements of the holy pre-existing historical manifestations of religion in the first place. Do we not come to know and understand what the mystical element is, for example, in the context of particular religions? Are we not made aware of the prophetic element by harkening to the message of specific prophets who claim to proclaim the word of the Lord? Again, his insistence that there can be no ideal religion of the spirit does not prevent him from claiming that what he calls the Religion of the Concrete Spirit finds its highest and most perfect expression in Christianity, especially in Paul's doctrine of the Spirit.[13]

We have already referred to the reawakened interest in the history of religions experienced by Paul Tillich as a result of his visit to Japan and his encounter with Buddhist and Shinto priests. The impact of this visit on his life and thought was tremendous, because for the first time he had come into contact with a religious and cultural way of life totally different from that with which he was acquainted. We noted also that he believed the future of theology to lie in an intensive period of interpenetration between theological studies and religious studies. Though time did not permit him to engage in a meaningful dialogue with the religions he had encountered on his visit to Japan (he died before it was possible for this to take place), he was able to initiate a discussion on the relation between Buddhism and Christianity based on his dynamic-typological approach to religions, and focusing primarily on the meaning and purpose of existence, or the *telos* of existence as he called it. He expressed preference for this kind of comparative discussion rather than one which simply selected contrasting concepts like God, man, and salvation, for the purpose of comparison. His Bampton lectures, given at Columbia University, New York, in 1961, and published under the title *Christianity and the Encounter of the World Religions*, included a Christian-Buddhist dialogue which applied the *telos* formula, and concluded that 'in Christianity, the *telos* of everyone and everything united in the Kingdom of God; in Buddhism the *telos* of everything and everyone fulfilled in Nirvana' [*sic*].[14]

Eliade speaks movingly of Tillich's contribution to a joint seminar on the History of Religions and Systematic Theology conducted in the autumn and winter of 1964, at the Divinity School of the University of Chicago, and of his grasp of the religious meaning and human value of unfamiliar myths and rituals, and his astonishing ability to analyse and systematize.[15] He refers to the seminar as an unforgettable experience, and it is his belief that Tillich was seeking a new understanding of systematic theology as a result of his encounter with the living representatives of religions in Japan, and that his creative thinking anticipated movements that were later to become popular.[16] Whether or not this is the case, or whether movements in this direction had already been anticipated in the writings of people like Troeltsch and Otto, is another question. As a colleague of Tillich at the University of Berlin, Troeltsch was influential in showing him the value of the kind of freedom that delivered man from the narrowness of the biblical approach and many other traditional forms of Christian theology. Among other colleagues, Rudolf Otto had initiated a dialogue between Christianity and Indian religions in spite of the theological isolation he experienced as a result of his activities; he, Carl Jung, and Arnold Toynbee were all equally influential in showing him the value of religious symbolism and comparative religion, and in providing him with a deeper understanding of the nature of the holy. There can be no doubt that the dialogical approach to the study of religions that Tillich embarked upon towards the end of his life, and that has come to assume such great significance and importance in recent years, owes much to the contribution of these scholars.

To return to the Bampton Lectures delivered at Columbia University, New York: Tillich recognizes that the exclusive attitude to non-Christian religions, which stresses the uniqueness of the revelation through Christ, had appeared continually in the history of Christian thought, but so had the inclusive principle. It had appeared in the concept of the logos as the 'universal principle of divine manifestation'[17] and had enabled Christianity to accept the metaphysical and moral principles of Hellenism, as well as the rituals of the mystery religions.[18] The exclusivist approach, however, denounced the relativist approach to world religions as a negation of the absolute truth of Christianity.[19] The neo-orthodox view exemplified this approach with its insistence that revelation be confined to the appearance of Christ, and its rejection of the attempt to apply the concept of revelation to other religions. Yet, as Tillich points out, Barth's radical exclusivism was produced as a result of his encounter not with other religions but with the demonic forces of German nationalism. The radical self-affirmation of nationalism in the form of Nazi-Fascism produced the radical self-affirmation of Christianity in the form of exclusivism. Barth may have saved European Protestantism by narrowing down his theology to meet the attack of Fascism, but, according to Tillich, Christianity paid a high price for this defence.[20] Exclusivism meant the rejection of theological openness and a subsequent blindness to the fruitful possibilities that might emerge from the encounter of Christianity with other world religions.[21] Dialogue between Christianity and non-Christian religions is only possible, he claims, when the attitude of radical exclusivism is rejected. The same is true, in his view, of the attitude of humanistic relativism characteristic of the leaders of the Enlightenment, which depicts Christianity as just one of the world religions on the same level as all the others.[22]

Tillich is convinced of the need for dialogue based on a

dynamic-typological analysis of the nature of the holy, the universal ground of all religions. He applies his dynamic typological approach specifically to the encounter of Christianity with Buddhism, which he describes as 'the greatest, strangest, and at the same time the most competitive of all the religions'.[23] In contrast with the Hegelian dialectic which classifies Buddhism as an early stage of man's religious development, the dynamic-typological approach regards it as a living religion embodying certain predominant religious elements which enable it to stand over against other religions in which different religious elements predominate. The interdependence of these type-determining elements provide the dynamic character of the relation of religions to one another, since they belong 'to the nature of the holy and with it to the nature of man, and with it to the nature of the universe and the revelatory self-manifestation of the divine', and constitute the perennial forces which produce particular religions.[24]

Dialogue conducted in accordance with the dynamic-typological method involves not only a discussion of the relation, or interdependence, of type-determining elements *between* religions but also *within* religions. Discussions *between* representatives of Buddhism and Christianity, for example, concerning the mystical and ethical elements in both religions, and whether one takes priority over the other, would be balanced by a similar discussion *within* each religion leading to self-criticism and self-appraisal.[25] True dialogue, in Tillich's view, can only take place when there is common ground for discussion, and a readiness on both sides to accept criticism. Furthermore, fruitful dialogue concerning the meaning and purpose of life, or the *telos* of existence, will only be possible when both sides acknowledge the significance and revelatory character of the other's position.[26]

The emphasis on the personal in Christianity and the impersonal in Buddhism is, for Tillich, indicative of the distinction between the two religions in their appraisal of the nature of reality. While the concept of the Kingdom of God is 'a social, political and personalistic symbol' concerned with establishing justice and peace, nirvana is 'an ontological symbol' concerned with providing an answer to finitude, separation, and suffering in the ultimate Ground of Being. It is evident here that Tillich's interpretation of the *telos* of Buddhism suffers from being subsumed in his idealistic approach to the nature of reality. His very use of the terms 'finitude', 'separation', and 'Ground of Being' points to that being the case. But his interpretation is as erroneous as the attempt of earlier interpreters to subsume Buddhism in Advaita Vedanta and the reasons for both misinterpretations may well have been the same.

Applying the symbols of nirvana and the Kingdom of God to the nature of the world, Tillich points out that Christianity conceives of the world as the creation of God and in its essence good, and man as a responsible creature who precipitates the Fall by his sinful actions. For Buddhism, on the other hand, the existence of the world presupposes, to use Christian terminology, 'an ontological Fall into finitude', and man is 'a finite creature bound to the wheel of life with self-affirmation, blindness, and suffering'.[27] It would appear that Tillich's predisposition to analyse and systematize leads him occasionally to misinterpret the nature of the religions he deals with, as appears to be the case with Buddhism, but it does not prevent him from insisting on the possibility of dialogue based on a typological analysis of the nature of the holy, or from recognizing both the affinities and distinctions that prevail between them.

According to Tillich, the dialogue between Christianity and Buddhism concerning the moral consequences of man's relation to nature and to his fellow man reveals specific differences. The ontological principles expressed in the symbols Kingdom of God and nirvana point to two characteristics, namely, participation and identity. 'One participates, as an individual being, in the Kingdom of God, One is identical with everything that is in nirvana.'[28] The implications of these principles for man's relation to nature are, in Tillich's view, profound. On the basis of the principle of participation, for example, it is possible, for man to justify controlling nature and using it for his own ends. On the basis of the principle of identity, on the other hand, no subjection of nature can take place, since man identifies himself with the processes of nature. Where Buddhist influence predominates the principle of identity finds expression. But the same principle of identity is to be found in Hinduism. There it finds expression in the prohibition of the killing of animals, which is related to the belief that in order to fulfil his karma a man may find himself reincarnated in animal form.[29] The implication here is that a man desists from killing animals for fear that he might be killing a reincarnated soul. But while it may be possible to draw such a conclusion, the concept of identity goes much deeper than that and, in fact, could be said to contradict Tillich's suggestion, which amounts to nothing more than enlightened self-interest. What the principle of identity really implies is the essential unity of all that exists. This is what prompts the deep feeling of compassion for the sub-human world and for all one's fellow men.

The difference of approach to nature on the part of Christianity and Buddhism does not mean that the two religions are diametrically opposed to one another on this question. In its mystical approach to nature Christianity can show an attitude which is almost indistinguishable from identity. Buddhism also displays a tendency to participation even though the principle of identity predominates. Tillich recognizes the existence of the Buddhist principle of identity in man's relation to his fellow man. Its main characteristic is compassion, which as an active form of loving can be compared with the Christian concept of agape. But in his view, there is a difference between agape and compassion. Agape, as understood in the Christian context, accepts the unacceptable and attempts to change or transform both man and society thereby exemplifying the principle of participation. Compassion, as understood in the Buddhist context, shows no impetus or desire to transform man directly, or to change him indirectly, by effecting a change in his social environment. Tillich concludes from this that even the most profound expression of compassion within Buddhism cannot be compared with agape because it lacks the power to accept the unacceptable and the desire to change man and his society. 'It differs in that it lacks the double characteristic of agape – the acceptance of the unacceptable, or the movement from the highest to the lowest, and, at the same time, the will to transform individual as well as social structures.'[30]

It is doubtful whether Tillich's analysis of the Buddhist concept of compassion is accurate. Transformation of individual structures takes place in Buddhism through participation in the communal life of the *sangha*, and transformation of social structures takes place as a result of the interaction of the life of the *sangha* with the life of the community surrrounding it. If what Tillich says of the Buddhist concept of compassion were taken to apply also to the Hindu concept of compassion, then his assessment would be equally inaccurate in that context. It can be clearly shown that the aim and purpose of *satyagraha*, for example, which literally means 'holding fast to the truth', and which finds expression in the philosophy of Gandhi, is to effect the transformation of social structures.

Tillich speaks further about the significance of agape when he refers to man's relationship with himself. He maintains that man's sense of alienation from his fellow men is simply an expression of his alienation from himself. The feeling of self-contempt that follows from his alienation from himself, together with the sense of meaninglessness and anxiety, indicates the depth of his estrangement from the Ground of Being. The answer to the problem of man's anxiety and meaninglessness, which derives from his sense of estrangement, is to be found through love. When love comes to him in the form of grace he has the assurance that he is accepted, and is thereby enabled to experience self-integration and the feeling of being reunited with others.[31] It is the ability of love to transform man's character in this way that distinguishes it from the Buddhist concept of compassion. But the same kind of reservation can be made about the distinction drawn between agape and compassion in this context as was made in the context of social structures. The removal of the sense of self-alienation and alienation from others is effected equally well through the Buddhist eightfold path and the Hindu doctrine of *ahimsa*. *Ahimsa*, which given its positive connotation means love, removes our sense of self-alienation; it binds us closely to our fellow men so that we are no longer alienated from them , or from Truth or God, or from what Tillich calls the Ground of Being. Similarly, right thought and right understanding, which constitute the wisdom aspect of the eightfold path, enable us to see things as they really are and consequently removes all forms of alienation.

Clearly there are dangers in drawing a hard and fast line between the principles of participation and identity. While it may be true to say that the one predominates in Christianity and the other in religions such as Hinduism and Buddhism, it would be a mistake to assume that Christianity is devoid of the principle of identity, or that Hinduism and Buddhism are devoid of the principle of participation. Tillich recognizes the former point, as we have seen, when he refers to the mystical approach to nature to be found in the work of St Francis of Assisi and the German Romantics, but he fails to recognize the examples of participation that derive from the communal life of the *sangha*, or the transformation of social structures that take place as a result of the interaction of the life of the *sangha* with the life of the community surrounding it.

Tillich continues with the dialogue between Christianity and Buddhism when he examines their respective attitudes to the historical process. For Christianity, history is the sphere in which man works out his own destiny, and also a process or movement which has as its goal the creation of a new society. This means that the Kingdom of God is a revolutionary symbol since its goal is the radical transformation of society.[32] Buddhism, on the other hand, with its nirvanic symbol represents a mystical, non-historical interpretation of history. No attempt is made to transform society in any way in order that justice might prevail for humanity as a whole.[33] Buddhism advocates meeting the ambiguities of life by transcending them, and its fundamental approach to history is to show how to escape from it rather than how to transform it. Even the new interest in social affairs displayed by contemporary Buddhists is determined by compassion rather than love.[34] The Buddhist emphasis, according to Tillich, is on the vertical rather than the horizontal as in Christianity. The same is true of Vedantic Hinduism which advocates escape from history into the blessed unity of *Brahman-Atman*. Not that this difference in emphasis precludes dialogue. In the same way as the horizontal emphasis in Christianity is balanced by the vertical emphasis in Catholic sacramentalism and Lutheran conservatism, for example, so also the vertical emphasis in Buddhism is balanced by the horizontal emphasis in Japan's acceptance of democracy, for example, and in the belief that every individual is of infinite worth in the sight of God.[35]

The criticisms levelled against Tillich's interpretation of the Buddhist concept of compassion apply equally to his interpretation of the Buddhist view of history. It would be a mistake to assume that neither Buddhism nor Hinduism is concerned with social justice, or with the transformation of individual and social structures, or that their main preoccupation is with escape from the world into the nirvanic realm, or the unity of *Brahman-Atman*. For the Buddhist, nirvana is capable of being experienced here and now, and the consequence of the Buddha's enlightenment was a forty-year ministry which set in motion the wheel of the *dharma*.

The fourth noble truth is the eightfold path involving morality, meditation, and wisdom, and resulting in the removal of desire, which is at the root of the world's suffering. This has implications not only for the transformation of individual stuctures but also for the transformation of social stuctures. Similarly, for Hindus like Vivekananda and Gandhi, their experience of God and their experiments with truth had profound social, economic and political consequences.

Tillich is convinced that a similar kind of dialogue should take place between Christianity and Judaism. The problems that emerge concern the advent of the Messiah, the role of the law and the question of reconciliation. Like many Christians, however, he has misgivings about conversion policies in relation to the Jews.[36]

Whatever the shortcomings of Tillich's interpretation and assessment of the Buddhist concepts he discusses, it is significant that he considers dialogue between religions, based on an examination of the type-determining elements of all religions, to be the most fruitful kind of dialogue possible. Religions participating in this kind of dialogue, he maintains, not only critically examine the predominant elements in one another's traditions, but also, at the same time, submit those elements to critical analysis within their own religious structures. In this kind of dialogue inter-religious appraisal involves the participating religions in a process of self-criticism and self-appraisal. That is, inter-religious dialogue presupposes intra-religious dialogue, a point we shall return to in the next chapter. Self-appraisal in turn promotes mutual understanding and a better appreciation of the basic unity of religion. Furthermore, fundamental to Tillich's dynamic-typological approach is the belief that revelatory experiences are universal and received by man in the context of historical, human situations.

Chapter Seven

THE DIALOGICAL APPROACH: HICK, SMART, CANTWELL SMITH, PANIKKAR

The response to religious pluralism which has emerged in recent years and found favour with many theologians is that which emphasizes the importance of dialogue. The dialogical approach, as we have seen, owes much to the contribution of scholars like Troeltsch, Toynbee, Otto, and Tillich, and is careful not to make exclusive claims on behalf of particular, historical religions. It seeks above all to cultivate intellectual openness and the spirit of empathy in one's approach to the study of world religions. It does not envisage that believers would forfeit their sincerely held convictions as a result of this approach, rather the spirit of openness and empathy is engendered in order that the adherents of different faiths might be encouraged to learn from one another through mutual contact.

One who is regarded as a notable representative of the dialogical approach to world religions is John Hick. He admits that the question of the relation between Christianity and non-Christian religions was one that he had ignored until compelled to face up to it after moving to Birmingham, where different cultures and faiths existed side by side. He came to realize that it was no longer possible for him to practice as a Christian theologian as if Christianity were the only religion in the world. This led him to develop a Christian theology based on a Copernican (God-centred) rather than a Ptolemaic (one's-own-religion-centred) view of man's religious life. He recognizes that the problem for the Christian lies in reconciling his total commitment to Christ and his awareness of the possibility that man's salvation might be effected through the teachings of other religions.[1]

His attempt to resolve this problem involves him in a

reformulation and reinterpretation of the doctrine of the incarnation. He advocates that Christ be regarded as a human being and not, as the traditional teaching of the Church would have it, as the second person of the Trinity. His view is that the incarnation should be regarded as a mythological idea and not as a literal fact. 'For if we continue to construe it literally we shall be continually handicapped in our attempts to come to terms with God's activity towards mankind as a whole.'[2] He develops his views in two essays: 'Christ and Incarnation' first published in 1966, and 'Incarnation and Mythology' published in 1973, the latter, according to the author, representing an expansion of the former. (The substance of both are incorporated in his book *God and the Universe of Faiths.*) The need for a Copernican revolution in theological thinking is made plain, but the problems inherent in such a revolution, in particular the problem of the place of Christ, is recognized as the most difficult problem for those concerned with the formulation of a Christian theology of religions.[3]

The problem referred to relates to what is meant when it is claimed that Jesus is both God and man, or is both human and divine. Hick suggests that in referring to this claim 'we might speak of the identity of divine and human activities of loving rather than an identity of substance'.[4] Not that this is an explanation of the assertion that Jesus is God, but at least it is an indication of what the claim amounts to. Hick's suggestion is that the language being used here is mythological, and he defines a myth as a story which is not literally true but which invokes a certain attitude in the minds of those who hear it. 'Thus the truth of a myth is a kind of practical truth consisting in the appropriateness of the attitude which it invokes.'[5] Attempts have been made to understand the incarnation as a theological hypothesis, according to Hick, but the lesson to be learned from these attempts is that the incarnation is a religious myth and not a theological theory. As such it expresses the religious significance of Jesus in a manner that has proved effective over the centuries. To say that Jesus is God, the Son incarnate, is to express mythologically the fact that God has been encountered through Jesus; the myth is an expression of man's experience of God. 'Jesus, in following whom we have found our way of salvation, and in whose shared life we experience the life that is eternal, must be called divine, Son of God, God incarnate: this was an appropriate way of indicating his religious significance'.[6]

The question that arises here is whether this proposed mythological interpretation of the incarnation sustains the belief that Christianity offers the only way of salvation, as the traditionalists maintain. In response to this question, Hick makes it clear, that since we do not suppose our own love or loyalty to be exclusive, or more authentic than other people's love or loyalty, we should not expect the same exclusivity of man's experience of God. The Christian encounter with God, therefore, does not preclude the possiblity of other encounters beyond the boundaries of the Christian faith. Hick quotes Troeltsch in support of his view: while Christianity has been the manifestation of the divine life in Western culture, other groups belonging to different cultural traditions encounter God in quite different ways. Other religions also make claims similar to Christianity concerning God's self-revelation and in each case the believers respond with devotion. It is appropriate, therefore, to assume that God has revealed himself in different ways, and the virtue of accepting the mythological interpretation of the incarnation is that it enables us to apply the same kind of interpretation to corresponding concepts in other religions.[7] That is, where claims to divinity are made on behalf of religious leaders in other faiths, the same kind of mythological interpretation can be invoked to explain them.

This brings us face to face with the question of the uniqueness of Christ. Is Christ the unique mediator? Does he reveal God in a way that no other religious leader does? If so, does it not follow that only those who have been saved by him have truly experienced salvation and that other claims to effect liberation from bondage are spurious? According to Hick, for the Christian to make such a claim would be dangerously dogmatic and as impossible to support as to refute. It follows that the concept of the uniqueness of Christ's saving activity might be interpreted as 'a particular redemption-myth attached to one great historical way of salvation'.[8]

The similarity between Hick's view and that of Troeltsch is clear. Both wish to preserve the possibility of divine encounter beyond the boundaries of Christianity and in different cultural contexts. Hick develops this point of view in his essay 'The New Map of the Universe of Faiths'.[9] He refers to religion as a universal dimension of human life and its history from its primitive forms to the status of great world faiths as a clear indication of God's self-revelation. The implication of this view for the relation between different religious traditions, and the truths they enshrine, is acceptance of the belief that the same God has revealed himself to man at different times and in different cultures. Man's response to God's revelation has, in each case, been determined by the characteristics of his cultural traditions as is evident in Islam, Hinduism, Buddhism, and Christianity.[10]

Acceptance of this concept of general revelation raises further problems concerning the conflicting truth claims of different faiths. Hick's response to this problem is to point to the difficulties involved in seeking to circumscribe God. Any definition of God is a limitation. It follows that we should accept the fact that different encounters with God are possible within different religious traditions, and that different accounts of those encounters can be given, all of which may be true, yet none of which would embody the whole truth. It may be appropriate in these circumstances to regard different concepts of God, such as Yahweh, Krishna, Allah, etc., as images of the divine, each contributing some measure of understanding of the nature of ultimate reality, yet none fully comprehending it. It is true that Christianity is a way of salvation, but other world faiths also are ways of salvation. The Christian experience of salvation through Christ does not preclude the possibility of other means of salvation. It may well be that 'they are all, at their experiential roots, in contact with the same ultimate reality, but that their differing experiences of that reality, interacting over the centuries with the different thought forms of different cultures, have led to increasing differentiation and contrasting elaboration'.[11]

Hick pursues this theme in other works. The very title of his book *God has Many Names* points to the need to recognize that God can be worshipped in many different ways. To a great extent religious affiliation depends on our place of birth, hence the need for a Copernican revolution, and a move from a Christ-centred to a God-centred theology. No world theology is possible if God is confined to the Christian tradition, or if we insist that *extra ecclesiam nulla salus est*. While it is right and proper to insist that the revelation of the Logos in Christ should be proclaimed to mankind, it is equally appropriate that other manifestations of the Logos in Mohammed, the Buddha, and the prophets, for example, should also be made known. What is needed above all is a move from a confessional to a truth-seeking stance; from exclusivism to dialogue.[12]

Hick's treatment of conflicting truth claims is examined further in his paper concerning truth and dialogue delivered at a conference on the Philosophy of Religion held at the University of Birmingham in 1970.[13] The whole purpose of the conference was to examine the relationship between different religions particularly in relation to their conflicting truth claims. He makes the point that perhaps we should seek to view man's religious life 'as a dynamic continuum within which certain major disturbances have from time to time set up new fields of force' which are 'the great creative religious movements of human history from which the distinguishable religious traditions have stemmed'.[14] The implication of this is that it is inappropriate to speak of the truth or falsity of religions since they are, like civilizations, simply the expressions of different human temperaments and different thought forms.[15]

If the classification of religions as either true or false is inappropriate, then we may ask whether it is possible for them to be graded in any way. In attempting to answer this question Hick looks first at the common ground that exists between religions, such as their attitude towards ultimate reality, human existence and the goal of life, then makes the suggestion that one might measure the extent to which religions either promote or hinder the goal of liberation, whether that be conceived of as the Kingdom of God, oneness with Brahman, egolessness, Moksa, or nirvana. The rationality of religious experience, or the morality of religious systems, might be examined, but Hick doubts whether reason or conscience are effective in grading religions. Internal consistency, and the adequacy of a religious system to account for the data of human experience, are clearly factors to be taken into consideration; but the fact remains that there are different ways of attaining liberation, such as knowledge, action and devotion, for example, each equally respected, and as far as morality is concerned no one religion is necessarily superior to another.[16]

Hick's openness to religious pluralism is evident and his attempt to grapple with the vexed question of the uniqueness of God's self-revelation in Christ, which culminates in what he refers to as the myth of God incarnate, is significant. He agrees with Maurice Wiles that the terms 'Christianity' and 'incarnation' are not synonymous and that the latter is simply an interpretation of the significance of Jesus.[17] He recognizes also that to regard such concepts as 'God incarnate' and 'the Second Person of the Holy Trinity' as mythological or poetic ways of expressing the significance of Jesus for us, has important implications for the encounter of Christianity with other world religions.[18] If the terms were to be taken literally, he maintains, it would follow that Christianity would be the only means of salvation since it could only be appropriated through Christ. But is not such an idea 'excessively parochial, presenting God in effect as the tribal deity of the predominantly Christian West?'[19] In Hick's view it is imperative that we see God at work in the whole religious life of mankind and that we view Christianity in this pluralistic setting. It would be most appropriate to recognize that different religions have different names for God. If we were to use the term Logos to indicate the means by which God effects salvation, then we would have to say that

> *all* salvation, within all religions, is the work of the Logos and that under their various images and symbols men in different cultures and faiths may encounter the Logos and find salvation. But what we cannot say is that all who are saved are saved by Jesus of Nazareth.[20]

We have already referred to the similarity between Hick's view and that of Troeltsch and his attempt to preserve the concept of general revelation in the context of different cultural traditions. His move from a confessional stance to one of seeking the truth, or from the exclusivist to the dialogical approach to world religions, is echoed in the writings of others. Robinson, for example, claims that to see things from a Hindu standpoint, serves as a corrective to a one-eyed approach to reality and truth; a challenge to exclusivism and claims to uniqueness; and a means of cultivating a wider vision.[21] Dialogue is necessary not in order that one religion might absorb another, like creating concentric circles, nor to show that religions are basically indistinguishable. The purpose of dialogue is to work towards an ellipse whereby, with the benefit of two foci, creative tension is established between religions and mutual respect engendered.[22] 'For to live in a society of competing one-eyed men represents an impoverished and, in an inescapably unified world, an increasingly dangerous condition.'[23] Hugo Meynell also considers the Christian claim to uniqueness to be wrong. In his view, certain attempted solutions of the problem of the relationship of different religions to one another are equally unsatisfactory.[24] This is true of the notion that each religion is true for the particular society it serves and that there is a close similarity between the elements of one religion and the elements of another, for example, the sacramental, mystical, and prophetic (an implicit rejection of Tillich's dynamic-typological approach).

Another representative of the dialogical approach is Ninian Smart, whose examination of the problems implicit in the relation of Christianity to other religions precedes that of Hick. He refers to the narrowness of outlook of modern theology and religious philosophy on the question of revelation and speaks of the shattering objections to be levelled against it.[25] Revelations are many and the question is, how do we choose between them? We cannot say that all great religions teach the same thing, or that formulations do not matter because ultimate truth is inexpressible. The persistent questions concerning the relation of great religions of the world to one another cannot be avoided in that way, and those who think about religion cannot really ignore the comparative study of religion.[26] If we ask, why be a Christian rather than a Buddhist, we are brought face to face with the question of the criteria of truth with regard to revelation. The advantage of dialogue is that it shows how great religions agree and differ on principles; it puts us into the other man's shoes. Apologetics, on the other hand, evade the rules of dialogue.[27] Among the many subjects that could be discussed when we engage in dialogue with other religions are revelation, rebirth, the incarnation, avatara and bodhisattvas, and the Trinity. Contrary to Tillich, Smart questions whether agape is so different after all from the Buddhist concept of compassion, a fact we have already referred to, and he asks whether we might not benefit from considering doctrines in a more Hindu way.[28]

The question of criteria of truth in the inter-religious context is examined by Smart in *Reasons and Faiths*.[29] He refers to the problem as a higher order exercise than theologizing, or engaging in dialogue,[30] yet he concedes not only that the truth of religious claims may be disputed, but also that the attempt to establish criteria of truth and the tendency to presume that there are genuine criteria may be misleading.[31] What emerges from his discussion of the problem is that it is not possible to establish a 'single analysis of religious language', or a 'single definition of religion in terms of content'.[32] There are clearly different strands of religious discourse which would be distorted by simple definitions of religion. That there are similarities between concepts is not in doubt, for example, God and nirvana, but there are also differences which are vital for a true understanding of these concepts. A distinction can be drawn between the numinous and the mystical strands of religious discourse. The numinous claim to justification involves an appeal to the holy, to the feeling of awe in the presence of certain features of the world which reveal divine characteristics. Justification of the mystical strand, on the other hand, involves observing the way in which the mystic lives his life. The question of the grounds on which one accepts a faith, therefore, is one that Smart considers important since blind acceptance would not be in accord with religious practice and might well be regarded as vacuous. But the type of reasoning involved in considering religious claims is of a special kind and differs from what is to be found in mathematics or physics. It follows that the normal distinction that is usually drawn between reason and revelation does not apply in this context.[33]

He pursues the problem of the truth-claims of Christianity and other religions and how they might be reconciled, by referring to the importance of the identification of truth-claims and their relation to what he calls *practice*-claims. The question he poses is whether there is a core of Christian truth-claims and, if so, how they can be identified. We work on the assumption that there is only one Christian faith, but there are many Christianities, and that the task of theology is to express this faith which assumes many forms. Similarly we assume that there is but one Buddhist dharma and one Islamic faith whereas there are many forms. The task of identifying the one Christian faith is made more difficult because of the many different models that exist. What we could do would be to recognize that the many different models represent different ways of expressing the one faith, and that there is nothing to preclude new theologies being created. It is possible that these new theologies might succeed in reconciling some of the differences that pertain between earlier Christian theologies and non-Christian theologies. The reconciling function of Christian existentialism in relation to Christian theism and non-theistic Buddhism is a case in point. It is appropriate nevertheless to relate truth-claims to practice-claims in order to prevent the indiscriminate synthesizing of religions.[34]

Can the truth-claims of Christianity be reconciled with the truth-claims of other religions by adopting the pluralistic solution? Given that tribal religions cannot lay claim to universal validity, and that different faiths are likely to continue, the pluralistic solution makes sense.[35] Tribal religions tend to be 'conceptually initiatory', that is, they tend to claim that God can be understood only through the experience of grace gained by initiation. Smart defines this position as conceptual fideism and maintains that as an account of the Christian faith it has to be rejected.[36]

The pluralistic solution, however, allows for the possibility of positing a single truth as the goal of all religions. But postulating an ultimate goal of truth involves identifying one religious goal with another. Is such an identification permissible? Do Muslims and Christians worship the same God? Pluralists stress the unity of religious experience, and experiential resemblance is established through the evaluation of the existential impact of the worship of God on the worshippers. But whether there is in fact a common core of religious experience has to be determined by phenomenological investigation and not by means of a theological a priori. Smart expresses the view that there is no such common core of religious experience; that there are different types of religious experience present in different religious traditions. It follows that it is difficult for him to justify the pluralistic solution, which allows for the possibility of positing a single truth towards which all religions aim. Not that the pluralistic solution is unattractive: but the incompatibility of religious truth-claims and practice-claims have to be accepted. Similarly we have to accept that each religion has a unique starting point. What the criteria are for resolving these questions of truth and practice is another question.[37]

Smart's reference to the numinous and mystical strands of religious discourse is reminiscent of Tillich's attempt to distinguish the sacramental and mystical (also the prophetic) strands of religion. Both acknowledge their indebtedness to Otto's *Idea of the Holy*, so it is not surprising that the resemblance between the two should be noted. The way in which they develop their analyses of these different strands of religions differs, however, as does the use that they make of them. What is significant in Smart's contribution to the dialogical approach to religious pluralism is his insistence that there are many revelations, many different types of religious experience and different strands of religious discourse, and many different goals of truth; this means that, in his view, the comparative study of religion cannot be ignored by any serious student of religion. It also means that dialogue is the prerequisite of religious studies, a fact that the apologetic and confessional approach tends to ignore.

Another significant contribution to the dialogical approach to world religions is to be found in the work of Wilfred Cantwell Smith. As we have seen, he favours a more personal approach to the comparative study of religion. We make progress in the study of religion when we recognize that we are dealing with people and not just with systems and institutions. Religion has to do with a man's faith, so the detached, objective study of religion should give way to personal dialogue. This in turn precludes the exclusive, proselytising approach, and fosters reconciliation and greater community. When the fellowship of reconciliation has grown sufficiently to enable the study of religion to become the study of mankind, then scholars of different faiths can join together to consider the problems of the universe which confront them all.[38] As we have shown, this is for Smith the prerequisite of any movement towards a world theology, which is for him the ultimate goal of mankind. A world theology would interpret the faith of all men in such a way as to recognize differences of form but not necessarily of kind. As Christians are saved by a Christian form of faith, so also Muslims, Buddhists, Hindus, and Jews are saved by their respective forms and patterns of faith.[39]

Smith's personal dialogical approach is clearly related to his stated preference for the term faith. The term 'religion', he claims, should be replaced by the twin concepts of faith and cumulative tradition, which refer to man's religious experience on the one hand, and the historical data of his religious life on the other. Faith is the impingement of the transcendent on man's life and his response to it, while cumulative tradition is a human construct which can take many forms and is simply the expression of man's faith. Religion, then, is the interaction of faith and tradition and it is important to distinguish between the two if confusion and distortion are to be avoided. The similarity between the distinction

Smith draws between religion and faith and the distinction Barth makes between religion and revelation is evident, and it is a fact that Smith himself draws attention to.[40] It is this emphasis on personal faith as distinct from the formal expression of faith, or cumulative tradition, that enables Smith to suggest that truth is located in persons rather than in propositions or statements;[41] to express his unease with the notion of 'truth-claims'; and to indicate his preference for the concept of 'bearing witness'.[42] It also enables him to make the point that man has to be a participant rather than an observer of the religious history of mankind; that progress is made in the study of religion when we recognize that we are dealing with people and not systems; and that statements about a religion are only valid when they are acknowledged to be so by the followers of the religion concerned.[43]

The personal approach is evident also in Smith's desire to ensure that any theological or religious theory that is constructed should prove acceptable to adherents of all religions. It is imperative, he maintains, that we should seek to understand other religious traditions, since it is no longer adequate for the theologian to work in isolation from the spiritual insights of religious traditions other than his own, if he is to avoid cultivating a ghetto mentality. Smith recognizes also the need to break down barriers and remove the obstacles that divide men from one another. Exclusivism, in his view, is characterized by arrogance and can be considered immoral. It is no longer permissible for anyone to say to his fellow human beings that he is saved and that they are damned, or that as far as knowledge of God is concerned, he is right and they are wrong. Such an attitude is morally indefensible. Christian theology must include a positive appraisal of other religions while at the same time holding fast to the revelation of God in Christ. Exclusive Christologies are unacceptable because they are a denial of God's love. We need to recognize that salvation is possible beyond the boundaries of Christianity because God is as Christ has revealed him to be.[44]

The significance of Cantwell Smith's dialogical approach, like that of Smart and Hick, is that he recognizes the need for the theologian of today to be acquainted with the insights of religious traditions other than his own. He rejects exclusivism, together with its accompanying apologetic and proselytizing mood, because it fosters a ghetto mentality and militates against the establishment of a world community and a world theology. When he classifies it as arrogant and immoral, he goes beyond what others are prepared to put into words. Not for him, therefore, Rahner's position of justified presumptiousness concerning the anonymous Christians of other religions, or Kung's proposed distinction between ordinary and extraordinary ways of salvation. He is at one with Hick in referring to exclusivism as contrary to the love of God, in noting the dangers of seeking to circumscribe God, and in recognizing the need to move from a narrow confessional stance to one of openness and dialogue.

Raimundo Panikkar's dialogical approach is not far removed from that of Smith. He proposes 'intra' rather than 'inter' religious dialogue and, as the term implies, he is concerned with engaging in dialogue from within, as it were, rather than from without. He speaks of intra-religious dialogue, and seeing the truth from within more than one religious tradition, as a stepping-stone to the renewal of faith. The basic aim of this kind of dialogue is to promote understanding; it is not aimed at conversion or the creation of a universal religion, but rather the removal of mutual ignorance and misunderstanding.[45] A Christian, for example, may say that he believes in God the creator, in Christ the redeemer, and in the Spirit as the pledge of eternal life. A Buddhist, on the other hand would say that he does not believe in God, that he knows of no Christ, and that this life is all there is. He would claim to believe in the Buddha, the Enlightened One, who has shown the way of liberation from the realm of suffering. For the Christian, God is the truth; for the Budhhist, no-God is the truth. 'Both have *faith* in the truth', Panikkar maintains, 'but for the one this faith expresses itself in the *belief* that "God exists", while for the other it expresses itself in the contrary proposition, "God does not exist".'[46] Dialogue may be possible, therefore, when it is acknowledged that the same faith may express itself in contrasting and possibly contradictory beliefs. It will be seen that Panikkar's presupposition here is that faith in the truth is the same in all religious traditions though expressions of belief may differ.

We may ask the question whether we can possibly understand the position of another if we maintain it to be false. The answer must be, in Panikkar's view, that we certainly do not understand it as he does, since he considers it to be true. For example, the

Vaishnava may profess Krishna to be the supreme manifestation of God and saviour of mankind. Can the Christian agree with this affirmation? It is not a question of either Krishna or Christ? Are not these beliefs irreconcilable? Genuine faith 'must believe those who do not believe' and seek to understand the culture, archetypes, etc., of others from the inside.[47] The distinction between faith and belief emerges again here. The Vaishnava's faith expresses itself in his belief that Krishna embodies truth. For the Christian to understand this from the inside he must share the truth of the Krishna of faith. Would this mean that Krishna had supplanted the Christian's belief in Christ? The same question could be asked if the roles were reversed. For the Vaisnava to understand from the inside he must share the truth of the Christ of faith. The basic question for discussion is the nature of the two mani-festations. 'While the Christian will say that Christ is the fullness and apex of God's every *epiphany*, the Vaishnava will be moved to say that nothing can outdo the *theophany* of Krishna.'[48] But it is possible for the difficulty to be overcome by mutual understanding, Panikkar claims, and true dialogue enables such understanding to emerge.

From what has been said it would appear on the face of it that what Panikkar is maintaining is that all beliefs are just expression of the same basic faith which effects man's salvation. But he regards that assessment as too simplistic, because he recognizes that there is no faith without belief. If that is the case, we may well ask whether it is possible for him to claim, as he clearly does, that the same faith may express itself in contrasting and possibly contradictory beliefs. The point he is trying to make, it seems, is that faith ought not to be confused with belief. It is the act and experience of a human being and is expressed in the images and symbols pertaining to a certain cultural tradition. This means that expressions of belief are necessarily pluralistic but 'in a certain respect they exhibit the same nature, which makes dialogue, and even dialectics, possible'.[49] To what extent beliefs succeed in expressing faith, however, is another question.

The rules that ought to apply in religious dialogue, in Panikkar's view, are: freedom from apologetics, a rule that would be heartily endorsed by other proponents of the dialogical approach we have referred to; commitment to truth; a readiness to relinquish a particular belief, or to be converted, if truth demands it; and recognition of the importance of the historical dimension and the social and cultural milieu of religious traditions.[50] Pursuing this last point, Panikkar makes the observation – and in this respect he echoes views expressed by Cantwell Smith – that any interpretation we might make of a religious tradition other than our own ought to coincide with the interpretation adherents of that tradition might themselves offer. For example, to speak of image-worship as idol-worship in the pejorative sense without seeking the view of the worshipper himself, is to introduce alien categories of understanding into a particular religious tradition, thereby trangressing the rules of dialogue. We have to recognize 'that there are no immutable categories that can serve as absolute criteria for judging everything under the sun'.[51] This point is not dissimilar to that made by Peter Winch, that in order to understand another way of life the onus is on us to extend our understanding rather than insisting on seeing everything in terms of our ready-made distinctions between what is rational or irrational, right or wrong, true or false.[52] We shall have occasion to return to this point later when we discuss the question of independent criteria.

While the principle of homogeneity has to be accepted, that is, that concepts can only be properly understood empathetically from within a religio-cultural context, it has to be balanced by the principle of dialogue if progress towards mutual understanding is to be made. As Panikkar points out, I may understand the world-view underlying the practice of human sacrifice, but that does not prevent me from considering it to be barbaric. The reason for this is that I am aware of a different world-view, or I have acquired a perspective which causes me to see the inadequacy of the world-view that supports the notion of human sacrifice. The dialogical principle is at work when we become aware of incongruities in our position and recognize our untenable assumptions. It is this that helps to create mutual understanding.[53]

For Panikkar inter-religious dialogue is unavoidable in the present climate, but he makes it clear that if it is to be successful it requires intra-religious dialogue, which implies questioning one's own beliefs, accepting the challenge of conversion, and critical self-examination, as well as seeing the truth from within more than one religious tradition. This notion of critical self-examination deriving from intra-religious dialogue, as we can see, clearly echoes what Tillich has to say about religious self-criticism and self-appraisal deriving from inter-religious dialogue concerning the type-determining elements of all religions and leading to mutual understanding. Phenomenological *epoché* then is not enough, that is, attempting to understand another religion, or engaging in dialogue, without involving one's own religious convictions. Panikkar calls it bracketing one's faith or setting one's own convictions aside while experimenting with another religion for the sake of the experiment.[54] Religious dialogue must be authentic in the sense that it must have no preconceived notions as to the result of the dialogue; that is, it must be genuine dialogue. And it must be genuinely religious in the sense that it goes beyond the mere exchange of opinions and accepts the risk of a possible change in one's religious outlook, or in Christian terminology 'a real, personal and ever-recurring *metanoia*'[55].

What this approach involves, as we have seen, is the total rejection of apologetics. Panikkar makes it clear that his ultimate aim is not Christian or Hindu apologetics, but an understanding of the problem and a readiness to accept the consequences of authentic dialogue, even the possibility of conversion. He claims to take Christ's affirmation to be 'the way, the truth and the life' seriously enough not to equate his significance with historical Christianity. Similarly his acceptance of the teachings of the *Gita* and the Buddha concerning liberation leads him to seek an encounter of religions that engenders mutual respect and makes mutual belief possible.[56] It is not enough, in his view, to use one tradition to enrich another, or to interpret one tradition in the light of another. True encounter of religions demands growth, which involves not only development and continuity, but also transformation and revolution.[57]

> In the contemporary scene where everything is in the fires of
> revision and reform, in which every value is contested and
> *metanoia* almost total, the authentically religious Man cannot
> shut himself off, close his ears and eyes, and simply gaze towards
> heaven or brood over the past; he cannot ignore his fellow-Men
> and act as if religion has assured him he has no more to learn,
> nothing to change. He must throw himself into the sea and begin
> to walk, even if his feet falter and his heart fails.[58]

Clearly Panikkar's dialogical approach as presented in this work goes much further than the approach of others we have examined hitherto although, as we have shown, there are a number of close similarities. He accepts unreservedly the consequences of authentic dialogue even to the point of recognizing the challenge of conversion following critical self-examination of one's own beliefs, and the eventual possibility of personal *metanoia*. This is what makes his intra-religious dialogical approach so distinctive.

His reference to taking Christ's affirmation to be the way, the truth and the life seriously enough not to confine him to historical Christianity leads us to examine his earlier approach to religious pluralism. He claims that God has not only revealed himself to the fathers through the prophets and in these latter days through his Son, but that he has also inspiried the sages of Hinduism and has been present in all man's endeavours.[59] The mystery that is present in Hinduism is what Christians refer to as Christ, but it does not necessarily have to be linked to acceptance of the historical reality of Jesus. The understanding of the mystery of Christ needs to be so enlarged and deepened that the doctrinal truths of Christianity on the one hand, and Hinduism on the other, are not circumscribed in any way, but rather seen as 'formulations, necessarily limited by cultural factors, of a more universal truth'.[60]

It is Panikkar's view that 'the spirit is suffocated when it is encapsulated', which is very similar to saying that when we define we limit. He claims that he is not seeking to 'dilute the Christian message or evade the "folly of the Cross" or avoid the Christian "scandal"' in any way. He seeks rather to indicate the existential nature and universal validity of truth.[61] When religious truth is so acknowledged mutual enlightenment ensues, and it is recognized that the relationship between religious traditions 'is not one of assimilation, or of antagonism, or of substitution (the latter under the misnomer of "conversion"), but one of mutual *fecundation*'.[62] As far as Christianity is concerned the ultimate divine mystery, which is both transcendent and immanent, is related to Christ. For Vaishnavism the ultimate mystery would be related to Vishnu. Rama or Krishna are other names that might be used to symbolize reality and each name, as a living symbol, manifests and expresses the ultimate mystery.[63] Christians, therefore, according to Panikkar, need to recognize the dimensions of Christ in other religions, and the main thesis of his book on the unknown Christ is, that when Christians believe in Christ as the symbol of ultimate truth they are at the same time drawn towards the same mystery that appeals to the adherents of other religions. For the divine mystery has many names and can be experienced in many forms, and each name or form enriches that mystery. For Christianity, divine mystery takes the form of the Trinity, and with Hinduism it is the concept of Advaita or non-dualism. So the divine mystery, which is the focus of the religious experience of mankind, allows for religious pluralism.[64]

If this earlier work lacks the more explicitly distinctive dialogical approach of his later work on intra-relogous dialogue, it recognizes, nevertheless, the necessity of accepting the universality of the divine mystery, which is the focus of the religious experience of mankind, and allows for the reality of religious pluralism. It might well be related to the concept of the Logos which, as we have shown in our examination of Hick's position, is revealed not only in Christ but also in Mohammed and the Buddha. That is, the many manifestations of the Logos correspond to the many forms of the divine mystery.

This more Christologically orientated contribution of Panikkar leads us to examine further the kind of response to religious pluralism that might be classified as Christocentric.

Chapter Eight

THE CHRISTOCENTRIC RESPONSE: THOMAS, SAMARTHA, DEVANANDAN

The approach to religious pluralism which on the one hand might be described as anthropocentric, and on the other hand, and possibly more appropriately from the standpoint of this investigation, Christocentric, is to be found in the work of M. M. Thomas. In his view, the common response of religions to the problems of humanizing existence in the modern world, rather than any view of God that they might share, is the most fruitful starting point for the meeting of faiths. He acknowledges that there has always been a variety of views concerning the nature of ultimate reality, but he recognizes that these different viewpoints have been brought to the fore in modern times by the elimination of distance and the creation of what might be called a global village. Dialogue between faiths is best pursued, he claims, where the problem of self-understanding and self-realization is examined and the ultimate meaning of human existence is sought. That is, intra-faith dialogue concerning anthropological issues has relevance for inter-faith dialogue.[1]

The changes that have taken place in modern society have been influenced in no small measure by modern technology, the growth of secularization, and the awareness within suppressed groups of their basic human rights. This has been accompanied by a spirit of self-awareness, which, in Thomas's view, has a spiritual dimension. While he shares Cantwell Smith's rejection of the term religion in favour of faith and shares his tendency to locate religious truth in persons rather than propositions, he recognizes at the same time the need to objectify religious truths in propositional form in order to evaluate them. He distinguishes two types of religious traditions, namely, the Messianic and the Unitive, which others – for

93

example, Otto and Tillich – might refer to as the prophetic and the mystical.[2] In both types of faith there has been a reinterpretation of basic beliefs in the face of problems posed by the spirit of modernity, and in man's struggle for authentic existence intra-religious and inter-religious dialogue has proved an important and significant issue. It will be seen that here Thomas has recourse to the terminology to be found in Panikkar's treatment of the dialogical approach to religious pluralism.

When he deals with the question of the relation of Christianity to other religions, Thomas speaks of the importance of recognizing the possibility of a transcendent Christ reformulating other religions from within. The point he is making is that if Christ is viewed as transcending Christianity as a religion, then it is possible to conceive of his transcendence being extended to include other religions, and their transformation being effected by their relation-ship with him. The theological possiblity of this transformation of religions is seen by Thomas to be implicit if not explicit in Barth's distinction between religion and revelation. While Barth, however, confines his reference to the possibility of conversion from unbelief to true religion to Christianity alone, Thomas extends it to include other religious traditions. Clearly Barthian presuppositions operate here for Thomas, and it follows that the same criticisms that were levelled against Barth can be extended to him. The uniqueness of the revelation of God in Christ is the *sine qua non* of both approaches.[3] This radical Christocentric approach which looks forward to the transformation of other religious traditions through contact with the uniqueness of the revelation of God in Christ, precludes the usual forms of syncretism and sees the quest for oneness being fulfilled, as Visser't Hooft points out, in the uniqueness of Christ, the centre of history, the one Lord, the Son of God.[4] Yet it does not exclude the possiblity of a Christ-centred syncretism which allows for cultural interpenetration and inter-religious dialogue leading to the transformation of other religions through contact with the transcendent, normative Christ.

What we have here is a form of exclusivism not dissimilar to that of Barth and Kraemer, and Thomas's acknowledgement of his indebtedness to both is an indication that he would not necessarily disagree with this assessment. Christocentricity for him, as for Kraemer, means unveiling the significance of Christ in the different beliefs of the peoples of the world.[5]

Explicit rather than implicit references to Christ are to be found in his book *The Acknowledged Christ of the Indian Renaissance*, which is a parallel to Panikkar's work, *The Unknown Christ of Hinduism*. But while the latter is concerned with traditional Hinduism and the unacknowledged Christ, the former deals with renascent Hinduism and the acknowledged Christ. Thomas recognizes that the so-called acknowledgement of Christ by modern Hindu leaders would, from the standpoint of committed Christians, be considered partial and inadequate. This would apply as much to Rammohan Roy's assessment of the precepts of Jesus as to Mahatma Gandhi's reference to Jesus as the supreme *satyagrahi*. Yet it points to the need for dialogue between Christianity and the contemporary religious and secular traditions in India.[6] It may well be, however, that Christian theology ought to be concerned with the creation of a true anthropology, or true human existence, since, as Thomas points out, men are responding to Jesus as the Christ when they acknowledge that human existence is grounded in love. This concern for authentic human existence may be regarded also as 'a protest against the restriction of salvation to conscious assent to a doctrine of Christ' and 'an attempt to discern the work of Christ and his work of salvation outside the Church'. If so it is, according to Thomas, welcome, but at the same time it should not reduce 'the essence of the Gospel exclusively to an ethic of love or to a mystic experience'.[7] It does seem that Thomas wants to have it both ways here. This is made more evident when he maintains that Christian theology should be concerned with the situational or contextual and should recognize that God's saving work in Christ is not confined to the Church, and that the dynamics of salvation can be discerned in such situations as the Asian renaissance.[8] What he is concerned to point out is that classical Christologies should not be regarded as permanently binding, and that the Church should be courageous enough to use non-Christian categories if necessary to reveal the uniqueness of Christ. Not that the Christocentricity of Thomas's approach is in any way prejudiced by this suggestion, however, since he believes that in the Indian context the Christian theologian is required 'to bring out new facets of truth and meaning of the Person of Jesus Christ and his salvation.'[9]

Paul Devanandan puts forward a view not dissimilar to that of

Thomas. For both, the transcendent, cosmic, Christ is normative, though not necessarily confined to Christianity as a religion, or to the Church as an institution. Both see the presence of Christ in other religions manifesting itself in the demand for justice and the desire to create a new humanity.[10] Devanandan recognizes that man is a fallen creature and that his selfishness is at the root of much of the disorder in the world. This selfishness is overcome, he claims, through faith in Christ, for as the radical renewer Christ inaugurates a new beginning for mankind. As far as the encounter of Christianity with Hinduism is concerned it does not mean the destruction of the latter; rather it points to its renewal and transformation.[11]

This Christocentric approach to religious pluralism with its anthropological overtones may be compared with the approach that emphasizes the significance of the Logos doctrine as the common ground of all religions. References to the Logos doctrine are to be found in both Pannikar and Hick, as we have seen, and it is also present in the reconception theory of W. E. Hocking.

A similar Christocentric view is to be found in the writings of Stanley J. Samartha. In lectures delivered at the United Theological College, Bangalore, in 1963, published later in 1974,[12] he was concerned with adopting a constructive approach to the formulation of a Christology in India which would take seriously both classical and modern forms of advaita philosophy. He was well aware that in so doing he might alienate both Hindu and Christian friends by undermining their cherished beliefs, but he felt convinced that such a task was necesary if Christian thinking was to have any impact on the national life of India.

He describes his task as a theological appraisal of the views of selected Hindu thinkers and an attempt to indicate the lines on which a preliminary, but by no means a fully-fledged, Christology for India might be formulated. He speaks of Christ as standing incognito in the midst of the religious, economic, social, and political life of India and of the need to recognize the evidence of what Devanandan calls the Christian concern in Hinduism. Traditional Christological formulations may be unacceptable to Hindus, but there has been a sincere love for the teaching of Christ, as comments of men like Gandhi and Vinoba Bhave show. This points to the need for a Christological formulation that would be in accord with Indian thought forms.[13]

Samartha describes the phrase 'the unbound Christ', which he includes in the title of his book, as an attempt to declare the universality of Christ and to indicate that he should not be regarded as the sole possession of Christianity. He points to its use by W. E. Hocking, who speaks of the unbound and unlimited Christ who pervades the world, as comparable with the Logos of St John's Gospel. The tension between universality and particularity is fully recognized, as is the question of the relation between faith and culture and the problem of religious plurality. Nevertheless, it is Samartha's view that the universality of Christ should not be inhibited by cultural or religious limitations. The implication of this is that Christianity and Hinduism should not be in competition with one another, or Hindus regarded as potential converts to Christianity. Rather Christians and Hindus should together, in fellowship with one another, seek the fullness of Christ and thereby contribute to the deepening of spirituality. Contact between East and West along these lines might contribute also to the possible emergence of a world civilization.[14] Samartha's basic presupposition here is that Hindus have need of the fullness of the revelation of God in Christ in order that their spirituality might be deepened and fulfilled. It is clear also that this is just another way of referring to the uniqueness of Christ.

In tracing the Hindu response to Christ Samartha deals with a number of modern thinkers who, in his view, are products of the cultural renaissance in India and representatives of the forces that have significantly influenced Indian life. Rammohan Roy, the acknowledged father of modern India, he notes, sees Christ as the guide to peace and happiness. Ramakrishna, Vivekananda, and Akhilananda paint a neo-Vedantic picture of Christ portraying him as the great *advaitin*. For Gandhi he is the ideal *satyagrahi*, while in Radhakrishnan's view he is just one of many *avatara*, or incarnations of the divine, and as the embodiment of human perfection fits ideally into the incarnational doctrine of Hinduism.[15] These responses, however, differ from commitment in the same way as acquaintance differs from acceptance. Samartha seeks a genuine Christology which could be rooted in the cultural heritage of India. This leads him to search for the hidden Christ of Hinduism and to seek to make explicit that which is already implicit in the Hindu tradition. He concludes from his examination of the responses of leaders of the Indian renaissance that a specifically Indian Christology would have to come to terms with *advaita* in both its classical and modern forms.[16] He cites Kalagora Subba Rao as an example of one who does just that, in the sense that he is committed to Christ yet equally committed to the Hindu way of life. For Rao, Christ is a guru to be followed, not a god to be worshipped, and needs to be liberated from the captivity of religion. His saving work should be interpreted in *advaitin* terms as effecting liberation from the bondage of egocentricity and *maya*, or a false belief in the ultimate reality of the world of the senses. The essence of salvation, from the Hindu standpoint, is to relinquish duality, and this can be accomplished through the kind of renunciation exemplified in the life of Christ. For Rao, therefore, the ultimate goal of life is mystical union with Christ.[17]

There are those Hindus also who commit themselves to Christ through baptism and yet remain true to their Hindu heritage. They include A. J. Appasamy, who endeavours to interpret the person of Christ in terms of *bhakti* with its emphasis on devotion and mystical union with God;[18] V. Chakkarai, who takes the humanity of Jesus into consideration in determining the essence of human nature, and sees Christ as the true *avatar* in whom the divine and the human are harmonized;[19] P. Chenchiah, who maintains that in Christ a new cosmic energy or *sakti* has appeared in the world effecting a new order of creation, and that liberation has to be conceived as having cosmic dimensions;[20] and Raimundo Panikkar, who equates Christ with Brahman, the origin, sustenance and ultimate end of all beings, the very ground of being, and who rejects the notion that the fullness of Christ can be 'exhausted' by the historical incarnation of Jesus and speaks of the unknown Christ of Hinduism.[21]

On the question of the prerequisites of an Indian Christology Samartha makes the observation that fear of syncretism should not be allowed to prevent attempts to formulate a new Christology where religious plurality is an established fact, for this fear might well have the unfortunate result of inhibiting dialogue between Christianity and other faiths.[22] Emphasis on the historicity of Christ would be of particular importance for an Indian Christology since non-historicity is generally considered to be a strength rather than a weakness in the Hindu tradition, with its stress on the *sanatana dharma*, the eternal religion. Not that the bare fact of Jesus Christ would be a sufficient basis on which to construct an Indian Christology; the social dimension of the fact would have be taken into account and its meaning and significance acknowledged and understood.[23] But no Indian Christology would be considered worthy of the name which did not take the highly respected and exceedingly influential *advaita* philosophy of Sankara into account. So there is no reason why the Church in India should not recognize Sankara in the same way as Aquinas recognized and appropriated Aristotle, though it does not follow necessarily that Christ would have to be described as the great *advaitin*.[24]

The way forward towards the formulation of an Indian Christology for Samartha is through *advaita*. The quest for Brahman, the ground of being, and for *atman* the essential nature of man, tends to detract from the significance of the historical world on the one hand, and the human personality on the other. The insights of the Christian faith might help to restore the sense of the historical and the personal in Hinduism, while at the same time the insights of the Hindu way of life might help to restore the sense of the unity of life in Christianity. Similarly the emphasis on transcendence in one tradition might be balanced by the emphasis on immanence in the other. Further insights could be dealt with in a similar way and Samartha's suggestion is that it is in the context of mutual understanding that a distinctive Indian Christology might be formulated.[25]

The Christocentric approach of Samartha to religious plurality echoes that of Thomas and is based on the same presuppositions concerning the uniqueness of the revelation of God in Christ. Dialogue is encouraged, but its ultimate aim is the formulation of a new Christology with a distinctively Indian flavour. The quest for oneness is envisaged as finding its fulfilment in an Indian Christology. If Christ stands incognito in the religious and social life of India, and if he is the universal, unbound, cosmic Christ, then he cannot be confined to Christianity as a religion, or to the Church as an institution, and there is no reason why *advaita* philosophy should not be adopted to express his uniqueness.

Samartha's emphasis on the importance of dialogue and his conviction that the major obstacle to it is, in the main, a fear on the part of Christians to meet adherents of other faiths in a climate of openness and freedom, finds further expression in a series of essays on the subject of the need for courage in dialogue.[26] He pursues his Christocentric approach when he refers to dialogue as a continuing Christian concern, the basis of which is faith in Christ as the Son of

God.[27] Religious pluralism, he maintains, should be viewed positively as offering different religious traditions the possibility of sharing new, spiritual insights, which might lead to their mutual enrichment. For example, Hindu teaching concerning the unity of all life, the Buddhist emphasis on *ahimsa*, and the Islamic insistence that inward peace derives from submission to the will of Allah, could only serve to enrich Christian understanding. The creative possibilities of pluralism ought to be recognized, especially the challenge it poses to particular religions to be less introverted and more concerned with the problems that face human beings everywhere.[28]

It is imperative, however, not only that dialogue takes place in the spirit of freedom and openness, but that the issues discussed should arise from the actual situations in which Christians and adherents of other faiths are involved. One of the crucial issues for discussion is clearly that of truth, and, in Samartha's view, the Christian has to beware of suggesting that his faith is true and others' false. Not that he should cease to be committed to his faith in Christ; 'freedom to be committed and to be open is the prerequisite of genuine dialogue'.[29] Dialogue enriches rather than diminishes one's commitment to one's own faith, but it also ensures that negative attitudes to other faiths are eliminated.[30] To define religion as unbelief after the fashion of Barth, and to include Hinduism, Buddhism, Islam, and the primal world-views in that category, cannot be justified.[31] But the question is how the particular revelation of God in Christ is to be understood. Samartha insists that 'the relation of the particularity of the lordship of Christ to other particularities should be considered not in terms of rejection but in terms of relationships'.[32] It may be possible for us, for instance, to recognize God alone as eternal and absolute, and all religions as relative expressions of that absolute. Our commitment after all is not to Christianity as a religion, since all religions have an interim character, but to God who reveals himself to us in Jesus Christ. We should not fear religious pluralism; what we need is the courage to participate in dialogue which might lead to the transformation of particular religions without necessarily detracting from their distinctiveness. For what dialogue really attempts to do is to understand and express the distinctiveness of one's own tradition in the context of the spiritual traditions of other faiths, and in the case of Christianity it is the question of the distinctiveness of the lordship of Christ.[33]

It is clear that Samartha's approach to dialogue does not envisage *metanoia* on the part of Christians. It is true that his approach is more open in this work than in his previous work, *The Hindu Response to the Unbound Christ*, which had as its aim the formulation of a new Christology with a distinctly Indian flavour, but his Christocentric approach to religious pluralism remains the same. His commitment is to the God who reveals himself in Jesus Christ, and the purpose and aim of dialogue from the Christian standpoint is to clarify the distinctiveness of the Christian teaching concerning the lordship of Christ. His openness, however, is evident in his recognition of the fact that the Christian has to guard against giving the impression that he has a monopoly of the truth and that the teachings of other religions are false. The same openness is to be found in his acknowledgement that one of the crucial issues for discussion, as far as the relation between Christianity and other religions is concerned, is that of truth.

The references to Barth and Kraemer in Thomas's work, and his acknowledged indebtedness to them, means that their response to religious pluralism, and that of Brunner, has also to be classified as Christocentric. The distinction drawn between revelation and religion, characteristic of the Barthian position, together with the definition of religion as unbelief, is in itself a sufficient indication of the Christocentric nature of their approach. The uniqueness of the revelation of God in Christ, as we have seen, is fundamental to the neo-orthodox approach to religious pluralism, thereby justifying its classification as a Christocentric response. The same is true of the response of those Catholic theologians for whom the fullness of grace and salvation is to be found only within the Christian tradition. For them, extraordinary salvation belongs only to those who believe in Christ. Recognition of ordinary ways of salvation and general revelation, mediated through religions other than Christianity, does not detract from the uniqueness of the revelation of God in Christ, and the extraordinary way of salvation mediated through him. It is evident that the Christocentricity of the response of liberal Catholicism to religious plurality is no more in question than the response of neo-orthodoxy. If there is a difference it is one of degree and not of kind.

From what has been said it is evident that the issue of truth raised by Thomas as one of the crucial issues for discussion in connection with the relation between Christianity and other religions, is one that has to be squarely faced by those who attempt to construct a theology of religions. It is tempting to enquire whether there might not be a criterion of truth, independent of particular religious traditions, that might be resorted to in order to adjudicate between competing truth claims. The problems inherent in the quest for, or in the attempt to establish, independent criteria of truth, will be examined in the following chapter.

Chapter Nine

THE SEARCH FOR INDEPENDENT CRITERIA OF TRUTH

We have discussed a number of theological responses to religious pluralism which have occurred in the recent history of Christian thought. They have differed radically from one another, extending from the Christocentricity and exclusivism of the neo-orthodox approach with its faith-religion distinction, through the dialogical approach of modern students of the history of religions, to the relativism and inclusivism of liberal scholars. The questions which we posed at the outset remain. These are questions concerning claims of uniqueness, superiority, normativeness, and finality for the person and work of Christ *vis à vis* alternative claims to uniqueness and finality in other religious traditions. This brings us back to our initial problems and to the question whether we are not led inevitably to the search for an *independent* criterion of truth, that is, a criterion independent of any particular religious tradition, whereby we might be able to adjudicate between competing truth claims. If we are prepared to recognize and acknowledge that a genuine and valid awareness of the divine occurs in all religious traditions, and that the love of God in Christ is not incompatible with the love of God in other forms, at other times, and in other places, then we are forced to question exclusive claims that might be made concerning the revelation of God.

What then, we may ask, determines whether a religious claim is true or false? What independent criterion of truth can we come up with that will indicate this? Christians may claim that Christ is the only-begotten Son of God while Hindus of the Vaishnavite faith might claim that Krishna is an *avatar*, or incarnation, of Vishnu. It is in the face of such claims that independent criteria of truth, unrelated to the religious traditions in question, would, if they could be found, help us to settle the matter. The following suggestions might be examined.

First, the claim might be made that the truth of a religion is verified eschatologically. But in response the point could be made that if it is the case that the truth of the Christian claim that Jesus is the only-begotten Son of God is, for Christians, its eschatological verification in the lives of believing Christians, does it not follow that a similar eschatological verification in the lives of believing Vaishnavites, of the claim that Krishna is an *avatar*, determines in the same way for Hindus the truth of the Hindu claim? That is, is it not the case that the same criterion of eschatological verification applies for Hindus as for Christians?

Again, if we make the principle of eschatological verification a universally applicable and independent criterion of truth, then we have to ask what sense can be made of the declaration: 'These truths we hold to be self-evident', where the use of the term truth is meant to show that the values concerned are to be regarded as the measure of truth? When religious believers make the claim that the truths embodied by their several religions are self-evident, then it is very difficult to know what independent criterion of truth we can possibly bring to bear on the pluralistic religious situation we are confronted with, that would enable us to determine which religion is true and which is false. If we were aware, however, that one set of truths for which self-evidence is claimed contradicted facts that we knew to be true in other circumstances, then would not that, on the face of it, imply that an independent criterion of truth had been brought into operation to falsify what are claimed to be self-evident truths? In one sense it has to be admitted that this is so. We can determine whether religious beliefs are confused or mistaken by checking those beliefs with what we know to be true in other circumstances. Religious beliefs are not immune from criticism because, as the self-evident truth argument assumes, the criteria for the meaningfulness and validity of those beliefs lie within religion itself. But, as D. Z. Phillips points out, it is one thing to say that religious beliefs should not violate or distort facts that we know to be true in other circumstances, but quite another thing to say that religious beliefs are justified or validated by those facts. To make such a claim is to assume that between religious beliefs and non-religious facts there is a necessary relation between that which is justified and that which justifies. To insist that what is considered intelligible in one context must be intelligible in the same way in all contexts might be regarded as an illustration of philosophical prejudice and an attempt to falsify the absolute nature of religious beliefs. The truth of a religion, Phillips maintains, is the confession of the specific content of that religion and we are concerned with intelligibility when we seek to bring out the meaning of that specific content.[1]

If we enquire of Phillips what is meant by the absolute nature of religious beliefs he cites mathematics as an example of what he has in mind. As we do not look outside mathematics to determine whether what is done in mathematics is correct or not, he maintains, so we do not look outside religion to determine whether religious beliefs are true or not. A distinction has to be drawn on the one hand, between 'checking' religious beliefs to determine whether or not they are confused or mistaken in the light of what we know to be true in other circumstances, and on the other hand, referring to this as an external criterion of verification or falsification. The former might be related to the concept of the unity of language games; the latter implies the notion that a single paradigm of rationality operates whereby the meaning a term has in one context is elevated to the position of becoming the norm of intelligibility for all contexts.

The second suggestion is that one might make morality an independent criterion of truth. That is, it might be argued that if immoral actions belie my confession of faith then my religious beliefs have been proved false by an appeal to the independent criterion of moral intelligibility. The suggestion here, however, is that we know what morality is apart from, or independent of, participation in a particular form of life. But can that be so? Do we not learn to identify what is right and wrong within a particular form of life rather than as neutral observers? We might consider some of the early practices of the Hebrews, for instance, to be barbaric, or some of the comparatively recent practices of the Hindus to be distinctly immoral, but might not their practices make more sense to them than, for example, symbolically consuming the body and blood of Christ? What their so-called immoral and barbaric practices indicate is the nature of their beliefs concerning God and the kind of activities they have been taught to consider right, and those they have been taught to regard as wrong. That is, there is a close internal relationship between their beliefs and their morality. If it is within particular forms of life that we learn to distinguish between what is right and wrong, then it is not at all clear how morality can be regarded as an independent criterion, or principle of verificaton, in determining whether religious beliefs are true or not. It may be necessary for us to recognize and acknowledge that there are different moralities and different religions which are grounded in different forms of life, and that attempts to regard morality as an independent criterion of truth, or the means whereby the validity of religious beliefs might be determined, are mistaken.

The third suggestion is that we might regard religious experience as a criterion of truth against which particular religious beliefs and traditions might be checked and assessed. It is precisely this tendency to regard religious experience as having a life of its own as it were, independent of particular historical expressions of religious belief, and apart from the historical context of religious language and tradition, that may have produced the revolt against natural theology in the first place. If we consider religious experience to be an independent criterion of truth then it might make sense for us to endeavour to construct a theology of religious experience. But is it possible to speak of religious experience in the abstract in this way? Does it not make sense to talk of religious experience only in the context of religious traditions? If we maintain that religions are true only when they clarify or illuminate religious experience, are we not making the assumption that religious experience has a reality of its own prior to, apart from, and independent of, the various forms of religious life and different religious traditions that exist in the world?[2]

The problem of establishing an external, independent criterion of truth is illustrated by accounts that are sometimes given of primitive cultures. Peter Winch, for example, asks what grounds we have for saying something is true or false, or does or does not make sense? He cites as an example, the Zande practice of consulting oracles. It might appear to us to be unintelligible, but it does not appear so to the Zande even when what we take to be contradictions occur and are pointed out to them. The question is, are we right and the Zande wrong? It might be argued that the Zande wallow in a sea of mystical notions while we in our turn are immersed in a sea of scientific notions. Which view is correct and which is mistaken and confused? Is it possibe to maintain, as

Evans-Pritchard does, that we are confronted here with two fundamentally different languages and two concepts of reality and that our concept of reality is true and the Zande concept of reality false? Winch points out that it is difficult to understand what true and false can mean in this context. What we are confronted with are different forms of understanding and different standards of intelligibility. In order for us to understand another way of life it is necessary for us to extend our way of life into the orbit of the other way of life. The onus is on us to extend our understanding rather than to insist on seeing everything in terms of our own ready-made distinctions between what is scientific and rational and non-scientific and irrational. What is to the Zande perfectly rational and intelligible, may appear to us to be irrational and unintelligible, but it does not follow that we are right and the Zande wrong. Winch's argument is that when a society has its own language and traditions, it also has its own concepts of rationality and intelligibility.[3] The parallels that can be drawn between accounts of primitive cultures and accounts of religious beliefs are evident, and it is clear that judgements concerning the truth and falsity of religious beliefs sometimes ignore the role played by such concepts of rationality and intelligibility in the different forms of life or patterns of activity involved.

Are we to conclude from this that there is no possibility of establishing an external, independent criterion of truth? Barth's position on this question is quite clear: the criterion of truth for the adherent of the Christian religion rests not in the inherent holiness of Christianity, or its morality, nor in the depth and profundity of the religious experience and religious self-consciousness of the Christian, but rather in the knowledge of God's revelation in Christ manifested by grace and appropriated through faith. Religion is never true in and of itself; it only becomes true through grace. Of itself it is simply man's attempt to know God through his own efforts and is in direct contradiction to revelation, which is God's self-manifestation through grace. The absolute criterion of truth, therefore, for Barth, is God's self-revelation. This is not something man discovers for himself; it is vouchsafed to him through an act of divine grace. It is an external and independent criterion of truth in the sense that it is the result of God's gracious activity and consequently independent of man's quest and external to his activities. Yet it is not an external or independent criterion of truth in the sense that it is external to, or independent of, a particular religious tradition or unrelated to a particular form of religious belief, and consequently it cannot be applied as a measuring line to other religious traditions in order to determine whether they are true or not. As we have already noted, Barth's view is that the truth of Christianity is not related to the fact that it is fundamentally superior to other religions, but rather to the grace of God's self-revelation, and the Church is the locus of true religion in so far as it lives by the grace of God. In Barth's view then, the fullness of truth for the Christian lies in the Christian message that the Word, contained in Scripture and proclaimed in the Church, is incarnate in Christ, and that God's self-revelation is the absolute criterion of truth. But how do we determine that God's self-revelation is unique in this instance and not in other instances? Is it the case that God's self-revelation in this instance enables us to state what is true and what is false and that there is no criterion of truth independent of, and external to, this particular form of self-manifestation? If that is so, what are we to make of the anti-Jansenist pronouncement of the Church *extra ecclesiam conceditur gratia*? If divine grace is believed to operate outside the Church then is it not the case that it operates in spheres other than the sphere of the Christian tradition, unless, as is sometimes claimed, it operates through the Church in its representative capacity?

Schlette also refers to the absolute nature of the revelation of God's saving power in Christ and the eschatological vantage-point of the special sacred history to be found in the manifestation of divine grace in Christ. It is this vantage-point that enables him to refer to non-Christian religions as belonging to the sphere of general sacred history, and providing ordinary ways of salvation, as distinct from the more perfect and extraordinary way of salvation of the Christian faith. Recognition of the significance of non-Christian religions does not detract in any way from the distinctiveness of the Christian faith. It is the self-revelation of God in Christ that enables us to raise the question of the role of ordinary ways of salvation in the first place, and to verify that they come from God. The salvation attained by means of the ordinary ways of general sacred history is in actual fact the redemption brought by Christ and mediated through the Church. This is probably what is meant by saying that divine grace operates only through the Church in its representative capacity. Yet while non-

Christian religions provide for a relationship between man and God decisive for salvation they are less than perfect, which is the reason why a transition from religion to faith is necessary in order that such imperfection might be perfected. Schlette's acknowledgement of the significance of non-Christian religions, therefore, does not affect in any way his insistence on the uniqueness of Christ. Like Barth, his position is that the criterion of truth lies in the revelation of God in Christ and in what he calls the extraordinary way of salvation of the Christian faith. Again it might be argued that this is an external, independent criterion of truth in the sense that it is independent of man's actions and external to his activities, but it is hardly independent of a particular religious tradition, or form of religious belief, and, therefore, it cannot be used as a measuring line to determine whether other religious tradition are true or not. For is it not possible for followers of those traditions to make similar claims for the gracious activity and self-revelation of God which has resulted in the creation of their religions?

The same view, though in a different form, is expressed by Kung. He does not go along with Barth in regarding non-Christian religions as non-revelatory, or as continuous with natural religion, or as specific examples of human autonomy in the quest for God. Nevertheless he does consider Christian revelation to be a manifestation of the plenitude of God's grace and non-Christian religions as serving a preparatory role in God's plan of salvation. The truth for Kung, as for Barth, is the fullness of the revelation of God in Christ, which, in Kung's view, makes non-Christian revelations, though they undoubtedly proclaim God's truth, nevertheless partial and erroneous in their witness. Like Schlette he distinguishes between ordinary and extraordinary ways of salvation. Only in Christ has God acted uniquely for mankind. Religions are structures which contain the darkness of human error as well as the light of revelation; they stand in need of the Gospel to liberate the truth. Kung denies that he is making a claim for the domination of one religion, yet he does not deny that the Christian faith lays claim to uniqueness and to possession of the fullness of truth. What has already been said on the question of the independent criterion of truth in relation to Barth and Schlette applies also to Kung. It is hardly independent of the Christian religious tradition.

Are we any nearer a solution to the problem of establishing an external, independent criterion of truth if we maintain that all religious traditions are relative expression, or finite forms, of the primordial form underlying all religions? Can we say that the mystical experience of the essence, or transcendental unity, of religion alone has ultimate validity and that all religious traditions are but relative forms of that experience? Or is Kung correct when he claims that such an affirmation is as much a matter of faith as the claim that God has revealed himself fully and completely in Christ alone? Is it true to say that the impersonal approach of mysticism is no less dogmatic than the personal approach of orthodox Christianity? Is the liberal theological approach as dogmatic in its own way as the more orthodox or neo-orthodox approach of conservative theologians?

As we have seen, Schleiermacher proposes that the transcendental unity of religion is necessary for the existence of positive, historical religions. These are concrete expressions of the primordial form of religion, which is experienced as a 'sense and taste for the infinite' or 'the feeling of absolute dependence'. This primordial form, or transcendental unity, is the essence of religion for Schleiermacher, and is not far removed from Otto's concept of the numinous, or Hocking's reconception theory, which seeks a better understanding of the essence that underlies all forms of religious life. While Christianity is, for Schleiermacher, one of the most significant and highly developed historical forms of religion, other forms are possible given different degrees of apprehension and receptivity on the part of man. Christian piety is just one form of piety or religion. The feeling of absolute dependence, or sense and taste for the infinite, is, in fact, presupposed in every type of religious consciousness and represents the finitude of man's being. The distinctiveness of Christianity, however, lies in the person of Christ who, by virtue of his identity with human nature and the potency of his God-consciousness, is man's redeemer. He expresses in his life the most perfect form of God-consciousness, which is why Christianity can be regarded as the most perfect and highly developed form of religion. Yet it is not the only valid or genuine type of religion; God can be contemplated and worshipped in a variety of ways and it would be irreligious of us to insist on religious uniformity.[4]

The question that poses itself here is whether this notion of a transcendental unity underlying all positive, historical religions –

that is, the primordial form which is experienced as a 'sense or taste for the infinite', or as 'the feeling of absolute dependence' – is, as Kung maintains, simply an affirmation of faith.[5] If it is possible to maintain the existence of a primordial element as the essence, or transcendental unity, or a priori condition, of all particular religions, then we have to ask the question – how do we go about isolating it? Furthermore, how do we apprehend this primordial form, and how do we determine the truth of particular religions by means of it? Is Cantwell Smith right to conclude that the quest for the essence of religion simply leads us further away from a true understanding of particular religious traditions?[6] Again, is Troeltsch correct when he states that historical investigation can point to no universal principle underlying the appearance of particular historical realities, and that theological works which refer to the principle or essence of religion as that which underlies individual religions, and Christianity as the absolute manifestation of that essence or principle, must be regarded with misgiving? Is he right also to maintain that such theological works elevate the concept of the principle or essence of religion to the position of a norm, while at the same time affording the modern discipline of historical investigation an inferior status? Is he right to claim that the modern study of history gives no indication that there is a progressive development from lower to higher forms of religious life, and that, contrary to Schleiermacher, there are no purely historical grounds for regarding Christianity as the most perfect expression of the essence of religion? If so, is he not also right to conclude that the attempt to present Christianity as the most highly developed form of religion must be regarded as untenable?[7] The Christian may make a religious judgement concerning the normativeness of Christianity based on his personal convictions, but he has to allow that similar religious judgements may be made by adherents of other religions based on their personal convictions.

It would seem that we are no nearer a solution to the problem of establishing an external, independent criterion of truth if we maintain that religious traditions are relative expressions of a fundamental mystical experience of the primordial form of religion, or finite forms of the essence of religion, than we are if we regard the self-manifestation of God in Christ as the ultimate criterion. The liberal approach is no more satisfactory than the neo-orthodox approach. Our basic problems are still with us and it may well be that the search for an *independent* criterion of truth to enable us to adjudicate between competing truth claims is itself confused and mistaken. If a committed Christian, in response to the question of what independent criterion of truth he would use to establish the validity of the Christian claim, were to reply that one has only to look at the lives of Christians, he may be betraying a complete misunderstanding of the significance of the question put to him, but at the same time he may be indicating how difficult it is for us to be neutral observers in the quest for truth.

The dilemma experienced in the quest for an independent criterion of truth to enable us to adjudicate between the competing truth claims of world religions is a very real one. Recent philosophical perspectives on the study of religion, however, may help us to see why it is that this search for an *independent* criterion may in fact be mistaken and confused. The Wittgensteinian approach to religious belief, for example, would refer to the absolute nature of those beliefs. As we do not look outside mathematics in order to determine whether what is done in mathematics is correct or not, so, we are given to understand, we do not have to look outside religion in order to determine whether or not religious beliefs are true. The criteria for the meaningfulness of religious beliefs lie within religion itself. We do not have to verify the truth of religious discourse by reference to an external criterion of truth. After all what kind of knowledge of the reality of God can we possibly have which is not already basically religious? To give a non-religious account of the reality of God is like giving a non-musical account of the reality of music, or a non-scientific account of the reality of science. When we affirm the existence of God are we not making a confession of faith rather than a statement of fact which is open to verification, or falsification, by reference to an external criterion of truth? But what if someone wanted to deny the existence of God in the first place? Would not this be in direct contradiction to the affirmation that God exists, and in such a situation is not some method of verification by reference to an external criterion of truth called for? On the face of it that would appear to be so, but, according to the Wittgensteinian perspective on religion, the denial of God's existence does not constitute a contradiction of the affirmation that God exists. Contradiction is not involved because the believer and the non-believer do not share the same mode of discourse. The denial of the existence of God is not a denial of a particular fact, but an indication of one of a variety of ways a person may stand in relation to the affirmation of belief in God's existence.[8] The givenness of religious beliefs as affirmations of faith sheds light on their absolute and necessary character, rather than their hypothetical character. That is, the fact that religious beliefs are affirmations of faith and not hypotheses accounts for their givenness and absolute nature. From the Wittgensteinian perspective belief in God is not a hypothesis which can be revised or discarded in the light of further evidence. We can say of things that exist that it is possible to conceive of them ceasing to exist. But believers cannot conceive of God ceasing to exist: such a thought would make no sense. Nor would believers ask of God questions they might reasonably ask concerning empirical things, such as, what caused them to come into existence and how long have they been in existence. According to Wittgenstein, the term 'God' is among the earliest terms we learn. We understand its meaning, he maintains, through stories, pictures, and catechisms. True, we do not see what is in the picture. That is, we do not see what it is that is depicted by the picture of God in the same way as we see what it is that is depicted by the picture of an aunt for example. What religious stories, pictures, and catechisms do is to introduce us to the reality of God. What we are presented with by means of these stories is an understanding or a picture of divinity and that divinity is the reality of God. When we understand the one we grasp the other. The fact that we do not see what it is that the picture of God represents does not detract from our understanding of the reality of God, because it is not the purpose of the picture to refer us to external facts, nor is it in any way dependent on external facts. On the contrary, it is the picture that reveals to us the reality of God and determines our attitude to external facts. We understand the reality of God through these stories and pictures for, as Wittgenstein points out, 'The whole *weight* may be in the picture'.[9]

From the Wittgensteinian perspective, therefore, attempts to prove the existence of God by reference to an external criterion of truth are mistaken and confused. When someone says that he believes in God, he is not making the same kind of statement as the man who says he believes that there is a chair in the next room. The proposition concerning the existence of the chair can be verified quite easily. The same kind of verification cannot be applied to the proposition about God because it does not belong to the same class of propositions. The fundamental mistake of Wisdom's parable of the gardener, whose God dies the death of a thousand qualifications, is the assumption that the same criterion of verifiability applies to both classes of propositions. The reality of God is not to be construed as if it is logically akin to the reality of physical objects. Talk about the existence of God cannot be equated with talk about the existence of physical objects. Neither can the question be asked whether we are referring to the same kind of thing when we refer to God as when we refer to physical objects, as if God were some kind of object the existence of which is capable of verification. If the concept of God's reality is to have any meaning at all it has to be found in the context of religious traditions since it is a confession, or expression, of faith rather than a statement in the indicative mood.[10] This is recognized, Rush Rhees maintains, when God's existence is referred to as 'necessary existence' as distinct from the 'contingent' existence of that which exists as a matter of fact. One can be mistaken about facts, but to doubt God's existence is considered sinful.[11] Wittgenstein makes the same point when he states that questions about the existence of God play a different role in men's thoughts and actions from questions about the existence of persons or objects. No one would regard it as wrong in any way if I did not believe in the existence of something or someone, but it would be considered bad if I said I did not believe in the existence of a god or God.[12] The unshakeable character of the proposition concerning the reality of God is derived not from its inherent nature, but from the role it plays in men's thoughts and actions and 'from its surroundings, from all the activities that hold it fast. Above all those activites involving the language of praise and worship'.[13] We are able to determine whether we mean the same thing by our use of the term 'God' by noting 'whether praise and worship mean the same thing for us, whether the same ideas enter into them', for it is in the context of religion, especially worship and praise, that God's reality makes sense. When a man says that God has become a reality in his life it is not that he has discovered an object akin to physical objects to which he is able to give the name God, but rather that his life has acquired a meaning and purpose it did not have before and which compels him to offer praise, worship and thanksgiving.[14] The problem, however, is that even when we have established that there is no single paradigm of rationality to which all modes of discourse must conform, and delineated the charater of the religious mode of discourse in question, that is not the same as establishing the truth of the reality of God.

A similarity between the Wittgensteinian approach to religion and the theological approach of Barth is clearly discernable. Emphasis on the absolute nature of the reality of God and the absolute nature of religious beliefs is similar in both cases. To an extent the same applies to their attitudes to natural theology. Barth draws a clear line of demarcation between natural and revealed theology. Similarly, the Wittgensteinian approach to religion would reject, for example, cosmological arguments for the existence of God on the grounds that they presuppose that the God whose existence is arrived at by the use of reason, i.e. the God of natural theology, is the same as the God who reveals himself by grace and is known through faith, though how the identity of the two is established is not at all clear. It might be conceded that cosmological arguments for the existence of God may have a certain value in making explicit the implicit grammar of religious belief, namely, that God is the source of the world, but can they be taken seriously as proofs for the existence of God? Nature is alien and occasionally diabolical, with living beings hostile and destructive to one another; its testimony is not unequivocal. From the Wittgensteinian perspective, therefore, the believer has no need to reason from the world to God since his attitude to the world is religious from the beginning.[15]

Where the Wittgensteinian approach differs from the Barthian viewpoint is in relation to what is sometimes referred to as the positivism of revelation characteristic of Barthianism.[16] The Wittgensteinian reply to any claim to religious exclusivism based on revelation is that there can be no philosophical justification for speaking as if there is only one morality and one religion. From the Wittgensteinian perspective, there are different moralities and different religions grounded in different forms of life and it has to be conceded, therefore, that there is nothing *independent* of different forms of life that enables us to adjudicate between them.

This leads us to ask whether there is any possibility of adjudicating between the competing truth claims of religions. If the search for an independent criterion of truth is mistaken or confused, does it mean that there can be no grounds for seeking to adjudicate between religions? It would appear to be so, yet the fact is that the existence of a diversity of forms of life in itself does not preclude the possibility of judgements being made about all forms of life from within a particular religious tradition.

There is, in the first place, the question of consistency. It might be argued, for example, that given the Christian conception of love certain attitudes ought to be regarded as unacceptable. This would apply as much to Christianity as to other religions. There could hardly be any justification for the use of force, for instance, to convert men to the Christian way of life, for that would indicate a greater love of dogma than of man. If it is argued that the end justifies the means in this instance does it not follow that the Christan concept of love is distorted? Inquisitorial practices, and certain missionary methods, might be considered unacceptable in this respect. Would it be considered consistent with the Christian concept of love, for example, if a missionary were to estimate how much it cost per capita to convert people to Christianity as if conversion were some kind of business venture? Not that the right of anyone to engage in missionary activity is questioned. A Christian may, even after understanding the Zande practice of consulting oracles, still want to change them, or put a stop to their engaging in this kind of practice. This is a matter of religious judgement, but the way in which the stop or change is made, and the attitude adopted in regard to them, could well be unacceptable and confused if inconsistent with the central values of Christianity.

Again it may be considered inconsistent with the Christian belief that man is created in the image of God to treat certain racial groups as inferior. Christian propounders of the doctrine of apartheid might well argue that, far from being treated as inferior, particular racial groups are being encouraged by means of this policy to develop their own culture and traditions with a view to establishing their own homelands. But whatever the long-term objectives of the policy of racial segregation, could it not be argued that in the short term it gives the distinct impression of being inconsistent with Christian beliefs about the nature and destiny of man?

The Hindu practice of infanticide and suttee, the self-immolation of widows on the funeral pyres of their husbands, may be considered by some Hindus to be consistent with their beliefs about *dharma* or duty. But other Hindus might regard it as belonging to a degenerate form of Hinduism and inconsistent with the teaching of both the classical Hindu tradition and the revitalized beliefs of reformed Hinduism. It would certainly be considered inconsistent with the kind of beliefs about the nature and destiny of man characteristic of the Christian tradition. That is, both from within the same tradition and from the standpoint of a different form of life, these practices would be regarded as unacceptable, though not necessarily for the same reasons.

Second, there is the question of factual correctness which could well be regarded as another form of consistency. People may be factually incorrect when they claim that only *their* religion has certain features. When they are confronted with similar features in other religions for which they claim uniqueness in their own tradition, they cannot really maintain their position with any degree of consistency. This has a bearing on any claim to uniqueness made within a particular religious tradition which might conflict with a similar claim to uniqueness made within another religious tradition.

The distinction that is drawn between revelation and religion is another case in point. (Although it might be argued that we are confronted here with a religious judgement rather than a question of factual correctness). It is a fact that, in the judgement of Hindus, revelatory features occur in the Hindu tradition, and a distinction is drawn between *sruti* (that which is revealed to the *rishis* or sages) and *smriti* (tradition). As the *Bhagavadgita* relates, Krishna, by an act of grace, reveals himself to Arjuna in a theophany which leaves Arjuna in no doubt as to the status of Krishna as an *avatar*, or incarnation of Vishnu. In the Mahayana Buddhist tradition the *Bodhisattva*, or Enlightened Being, is presented as having all the characteristics of a Saviour. In view of the similarities of these revelatory features in different religious traditions might it not be considered arbitrary on the part of certain Christian theologians to classify religion (as distinct from revelation) as unbelief, or as man's futile attempt to reach God, as if revelation itself is somehow unrelated to specific religious traditions, and also to insist that there is but one Saviour for all men?

Yet while there may be certain grounds for adjudicating between religions when it comes to discussing questions of consistency and factual correctness, the fact remains that as far as competing truth claims are concerned, as we have seen, there appears to be no criterion of truth independent of the different religious traditions, to enable us to adjudicate between them, and that the quest for an independent criterion of truth is itself mistaken and confused. The fact that there are different moralities and different religions grounded in different forms of life is clearly something that the Christian theologian has to bear in mind as he seeks to formulate a theology of religions.

Chapter Ten

AN ASSESSMENT OF THE RESPONSES TO PLURALITY

The unsuccessful quest for independent criteria of truth to enable us to adjudicate between competing truth claims leads us to a further examination and analysis of the different theological responses to religious pluralism that have been made in the recent history of Christian thought, and that we have dealt with hitherto in this study. We might begin by seeking to assess the claim made for the uniqueness of Christianity based on the once-and-for-allness of the revelation of God in Christ.

THE UNIQUENESS OF CHRISTIANITY

We have seen that the claim to exclusiveness made for the revelation of God in Christ is the primary characteristic of the neo-orthodox response of Barth. In support of this claim a distinction is drawn between religion and faith, and the concept of revelation is confined to that which occurs as a result of the gracious self-manifestation of God through the Word incarnate in Christ. In the essence of his nature God is inscrutable to man; he is the *Deus absconditus*. There is no possibility of man discovering God by his own efforts, no matter how spiritually enlightened, or intellectually sophisticated, or erudite he might be, because there is simply no bridge from man to God. There is no such thing as natural theology because there is discontinuity rather than continuity between God's self-revelation and man's religious discovery. The revelation of God in Christ cannot be regarded as an extension of man's religion, which is simply man's arrogant and futile attempt to come to know God by his own efforts. Religion is indicative of man's unbelief in the sense that he refuses to believe or to accept that it is only through God's initiative in his self-revelation that the *Deus absconditus* has become the *Deus revelatus*. Lest it be thought that Christianity as a religion is exempt from Barth's general indictment of religion, he points out, as we have seen, that Christianity is only considered to be a true religion when it is justified and sanctified by revelation. That is to say, it is a true religion when it is the locus of faith. Should it ever be tempted to consider itself superior, or seek to lay claim to a position of privilege among the religions of the world for other reasons, such as possessing superior religious experience, or a deeper sense of holiness than other religions, then it forfeits its claim to be the locus of faith.

The question that arises as a consequence of the stark distinction that is drawn between religion and faith, and the fact that the concept of revelation is confined to God's self-disclosure through the Word incarnate in Christ, is this: what are we to make of the the claims of other religions to be recipients of God's revelation? Is it enough simply to dismiss these claims out of hand as confused or mistaken? Are all those non-Christian religious leaders misguided who claim to have received revelation from God? Was Mohammed mistaken in his beliefs, and are his followers misguided in believing him to be a genuine prophet of Allah? What is it about the revelation of God in Christ that makes it different in kind and not simply in degree from other non-Christian revelations? What is it about the biblically attested revelation of God in Christ that makes it unique? How do we determine that revelation is unique in this instance and not in other instances? The reply might be that this is a religious judgement, or an illustration of what Tillich calls the daring courage of the Christian faith. That is, it is a confession of faith and as such stands in no need of external verification. The absolute criterion of truth for the Christian is to be found in God's self-revelation. If this is the case, what is there to prevent the adherents of other religions from making similar religious judgements about the revelation of God contained in their traditions? And why should they not also refer to their claims to uniqueness as illustrations of the daring courage of their faiths? On the face of it there would appear to be nothing to prevent them from doing just that, which means that we are left with a choice between different religious judgements concerning what is considered to be unique. What has to be avoided in each case, it would seem, is the danger of equating what is ostensibly a religious judgement with a statement of fact.

On the basis of the religious judgement, or confession of faith, that the revelation of God in Christ is unique, it is perfectly understandable that Christians should wish to engage in missionary activity in order to bring to the knowledge of the fullness of the revelation of God, those whom they consider to be languishing in the darkness of unbelief, even the unbelief of religion. But what if the so-called darkness of religious unbelief is the light of faith for adherents of other religious traditions? That is, what if the adherents of those non-Christian religious traditions refuse to accept the Christian claim, and in their turn engage in missionary activity? Why should their attempt to bring others to the faith that God has revealed to them, or to their understanding of the nature of reality be less acceptable than the attempts of Christians? What is involved here after all is a difference of judgement concerning the nature of revelation and, as we have seen, the attempt to establish an independent criterion of truth to enable us to adjudicate between competing truth claims is both mistaken and confused.

The claim for the uniqueness of the revelation of God in Christ takes a different form in the work of Brunner. In the first place he does not make the same distinction between religion and faith as Barth does. In his view, there is general revelation both in the works of creation and in the spiritual insights of religious traditions other than Christianity. General revelation ensures that man is made aware of his relation to God and thereby made responsible for his actions. But this does not detract from the uniqueness of the redemptive power of the revelation in Christ. In itself general revelation has no saving significance, and this applies as much to primitive, polytheistic, and mystical religions, including Buddhism, as it does to the works of creation. There is a difference, however, to be noted in relation to the prophetic religions which can lay claim to be based on authentic revelation. Yet, according to Brunner, even they lack redemptive qualities or saving grace and, therefore, do not compare with the uniqueness of the self-revelation of God in Christ. It is evident that the uniqueness of the Christian revelation is preserved in Brunner though not in the same way as in Barth. Since for Brunner God has never left himself without a witness, both creation and the spiritual insights of other religions point to his revelation, which finds its fulfilment in God's self-disclosure in Christ.

The question that has to be faced is why is it that general revelation in creation, and in the spiritual insights of other religions, lack saving significance? Furthermore, why should such revelation make man responsible for his actions and aware of his tendency to sinfulness and apostasy, yet stop short of providing him with the means to overcome it? It is the same God, according to Brunner, who reveals himself through creation as speaks to man through the incarnate Christ. Why is it then that God is reticent to save in one instance and not in another? Again, on what grounds is Brunner able to determine that there is no salvation through other religions and that the revelation of God in Christ is unique? Is this what is meant by saying that the claim for the uniqueness of the Christian faith is a religious judgement, or an example of the daring courage of the Christian faith, rather than a statement in the indicative mood? If so what is to prevent a similar religious judgement being made by adherents of religions other than Christianity for the uniqueness of their faiths, or for the claim to uniqueness to be made by different religons in turn in order to illustrate the daring courage of their faiths? Given the absence of any external criterion of truth to enable us to adjudicate, and bearing in mind what has already been said about the absolute nature of religious beliefs, it would appear that there is nothing to prevent claims to uniqueness being made by different religious traditions. As far as Brunner is concerned, however, Christianity's claim to uniqueness lies in the redemptive quality of God's self-disclosure in Christ as compared with the lack of saving power in non-Christian revelations. For Barth, on the other hand, revelation is confined to the self-disclosure of God in the incarnate Word, and Christianity's sole claim to uniqueness lies in its witness to God's self-revelation.

Hendrik Kraemer shares with Barth and Brunner their belief in the uniqueness of the revelation of God in Christ. It is primarily God's self-disclosure to man and points to the discontinuity of nature and grace. He parts company with Barth, however, on the question of general revelation on the grounds that God does not abandon the work of his hands and that the world is still his creation. Yet he does not believe we can say that the difference between general revelation and the revelation of God in Christ is simply one of degree and not of kind. Neither can we say that general revelation is a preparation for the fullness of revelation in Christ. What can be said is that we truly understand general revelation in the light of the special revelation of God in Christ. As far as Kraemer is concerned, and here he is at one with Barth, the ultimate criterion of truth is the fact of Christ. There is a radical distinction between religion and revelation and the one distinctive and unique element in Christianity is God's revelation in Christ. Without it Christianity must be regarded as a religion just like other religions, and as such indicative of man's futile quest for God. Since there is a distinction to be drawn between religion and revelation it is nonsense to say that Christianity, regarded simply as a religion, is true and other religions false. The fact is, according to Kraemer, there is no true religion as such. Only the revelation of God in Christ is true. The absolute criterion of truth is the fact of Christ, who differs from other religious leaders like Mohammed or the Buddha in that he embodies revelation in his own person. On the whole, therefore, there is little to distinguish Kraemer's viewpoint from that of Barth and Brunner on the question of the uniqueness of God's revelation in Christ, though, as we have seen, he is closer to Brunner than to Barth on the question of general revelation. Yet the distinction that he draws between religion and revelation puts him closer to Barth and seems to indicate that, despite what he has to say about general revelation, redemptive revelation is confined to the Christian faith. The questions posed concerning the positions of Barth and Brunner apply equally to Kraemer, and given that we have no recourse to a criterion of truth independent of the religious traditions concerned, it would seem that we are no nearer a resolution of the problem of the Christian claim to uniqueness based on the self-disclosure of God in Christ. If what we have here is a confession of faith, or a religious judgement, then there would appear to be nothing to prevent adherents of other religious traditions from making similar confessions of faith and laying similar claims to uniqueness if they so wished.

Such a claim to uniqueness, or what appears to be something close to it, is to be found in the writings of one of the major influential figures in the history of modern India, namely, Dayananda Saraswati. His concern for the authoritative source of Hinduism leads him to maintain that Vedic revelation as contained in the four Vedas is the only true revelation. For him the four Vedas constitute the Word of God and are the repository of religious truth and knowledge. They are

> absolutely free from error and are an authority unto themselves. In other words, they do not stand in need of any other book to uphold their authority. Just as the sun (or a lamp) by its light, reveals its own nature as well as that of other objects of the universe, such as the earth – even so are the *Vedas*.[1]

As Kraemer points to the fact of Christ as the absolute criterion of truth, so in the same way does Dayananda point to the Vedas as 'the supreme authority in the ascertainment of true religion' and goes on to maintain that what is enjoined by them is right and what is condemned by them is wrong. According to Dayananda, all men 'should believe in the *Vedas* and thereby cultivate unity in religion'.[2] He defends this view vigorously against the more pluralistic views of his contemporary, Keshab Chunder Sen, and by means of the society he founded, the Arya Samaj, he seeks to promote the authority of the Vedas as the source of God's true revelation. He advocates also a rigorous monotheism that eschews all representations of the Divine even to the extent of regarding *avatara* or incarnations as idolatrous. Since God is formless he cannot have an image [3] and since he is unborn he cannot take on a human form.[4] From Dayananda's standpoint, therefore, Christianity must be considered idolatrous because it upholds belief in the incarnation of God in Christ, a doctrine that

> cannot stand even the test of reasoning, for He, who pervades the universe like ether, is Infinite, Invisible, and is not susceptible to pleasure and pain, cannot be contained in a drop of semen or in the uterus or in a bodily tenement.[5]

Certain Hindu practices are also considered idolatrous and contrary to Vedic teaching. In fact, according to Dayananda, idol worship is responsible for those 'idle, lazy, indolent, and beggarly priests in India, who are mainly answerable for this widespread ignorance, fraud and mendacity in the country'.[6] It will be evident from the distinction that is being drawn here between revelation and religious practices that, like Barth, Dayananda is subjecting religion, even his own Hindu religion, to the judgement of revelation, although for him it is Vedic revelation rather than the self-revelation of God in Christ.

In view of this emphasis on the uniqueness of Vedic revelation we may ask whether it is the case that what we have here is a religious judgement, or an expression of the daring courage of a particular form of the Hindu faith? If this confession of faith in the uniqueness of Vedic revelation stands in need of no external verification, or to use Dayananda's words, if the Vedas are the Word of God, and an authority unto themselves, requiring no other books to uphold that authority, then, as we have previously indicated, what we are left with is a choice between different religious judgements as to what is to be regarded as unique. Furthermore, on the basis of the religious judgement that the revelation of God in the Vedas is the only true revelation, would it not have to be acknowledged that the members of the Arya Samaj, who uphold this belief, have the same right as adherents of other religious traditions to bring to the knowledge of the fullness of the revelation of God, those whom they considered to be languishing in the darkness of mythology and idolatry? That is, can it not be maintained with some justification that missionary activity is not to be considered the prerogative of one religious tradition to the exclusion of all others? For, as we have tried to show, it is a matter of choice between different religious judgements, doubtless influenced in no small measure by the particular religious tradition in which a person is nurtured and which determines his way of life, whether he considers true revelation to be located in the fact of Christ or in the Vedas.

THE FINALITY AND NORMATIVENESS
OF CHRISTIANITY

A further response to religious pluralism, as we have seen, is the claim that Christianity is the fulfilment of man's religious development and the culmination of God's revelation. While it is undoubtedly true that God reveals himself to man in religions other than Christianity, his revelation in those traditions, according to this view, must be regarded as preparatory. His final revelation to man is given through Christ alone; it is only within the Christian tradition that the fullness and plenitude of revelatory grace is to be found.

The distinction drawn between God's preparatory and final revelation takes different forms. One form is found in Kung's claim that universal salvation history as exemplified through non-Christian religions is distinct from special salvation history which is revealed through Christ. Both are the result of God's grace, but the former provide ordinary ways of salvation as distinct from the extraordinary way of salvation that is available to man only through Christ. It is evident that the finality and normativeness of the revelation of God in Christ is preserved by means of this distinction. Although Kung rejects as a theological fabrication designed to sweep men of good will into the Catholic Church by the back door, the classification of recipients of God's grace as anonymous Christians, he still maintains that non-Christian religions do not offer the fullness of truth. For him, the finality of the revelation of God in Christ is still a fact that he finds it difficult to relinquish. It may well be that the distinction between preparatory and final revelation may not be a distinction between different kinds of revelation, since God is the source of both, but there is without doubt a major difference of degree. We may not have here the stark distinction between religion and revelation so characteristic of the neo-orthodox response to religious pluralism, but the difference of degree between preparatory and final revelation is such that it still makes Christianity distinctive. Kung emphasizes the need for a theocentric as opposed to an ecclesio-centric approach to religious plurality in order that there might be a more positive assessment of non-Christian religions; despite this it is quite clear that, as far as he is concerned, non-Christian religions do not offer the fullness of truth and that they stand in need of the Gospel before true communion between man and God can take place. In view of this his claim to favour dialogue can hardly be taken to mean open-ended dialogue.

Another form of the distinction between preparatory and final revelation is that to be found in Schlette's reference to general sacred history as distinct from special sacred history. The former is positively willed by God and provides the ground for the ordinary ways of salvation of non-Christian religions. But general sacred history is fulfilled by special sacred history which is the occasion of the extraordinary way of salvation provided by the revelation of God in Christ. The similarity between the positions of Schlette and Kung on this point is apparent, but Schlette goes further when he explicitly refers to the extraordinary way of salvation through Christ as definitive and perfect, and ordinary ways of salvation as imperfect. It is in the light of the normative or definitive extraordinary way of salvation through Christ that ordinary ways of salvation through non-Christian religions are judged in the first place, and verified as coming from God. Furthermore, since ordinary ways of salvation are imperfect there has to be a transition, or conversion, from non-Christian religions to the Christian faith in order that imperfection might be perfected. Recognition of the value of non-Christian religions, therefore, does not detract in any way from the finality and normativeness of the Christian faith as far as Schlette is concerned. Like Kung, he insists that they do not offer the fullness of truth and that they stand in need of the normative, definitive, extraordinary way of salvation through Christ for truth to be liberated and fully revealed.

A further form of the distinction between preparatory and final revelation is that to be found in Rahner's position, which describes members of non-Christian religions as anonymous Christians and the Church as the vanguard, or explicit expression, of that hidden reality that is inherent in all non-Christian religions. Rahner's point is that all men are the recipients of God's revelatory grace. But since it is the Catholic view that there is no salvation apart from Christ, then it follows that, if members of non-Christian religions have experienced salvation through God's grace, they must inevitably be regarded as anonymous Christians, or Christians incognito. No matter how presumptuous this position might appear to be from the standpoint of non-Christians, and as we have seen from Kung's point of view also, according to Rahner no other position can be considered acceptable to the Catholic Christian if he wishes to uphold the finality and uniqueness of Christianity. If the fullness of truth, and the completeness and finality of revelation, is only possible through the revelation of God in Christ, then the Gospel must be proclaimed in order to make manifest the hidden reality of that anonymous form of Christianity implicit in non-Christian religions. The preparatory nature of non-Christian revelation, therefore, lies in the fact that man is capable of being a *homo religiousus* in the context of the religious situation in which he has been nurtured and which has determined his way of life, and that God's saving purpose is made known to him through his own religious tradition. A more explicit awareness of God's saving purpose, however, and a greater knowledge of the truth is only made possible through the proclamation of the Gospel, that is, through the fullness of the revelation of God in Christ. As far as Rahner is concerned, recognition of the value of non-Christian religions as anonymous forms of Christianity does not detract from the uniqueness of Christianity, or the finality of the Christian revelation. For him, as for Kung and Schlette, Christianity is the only true religion and as such essential for man's salvation.

Another form of the distinction between preparatory and final revelation is to be found in what Tillich has to say about *kairos* and *kairoi*. He makes the point, as we have seen, that while there are *kairoi*, or momentous events, of great religious significance in the history of religions, the central event which is of universal significance, is the *kairos*, or the momentous event, of the appearance of Jesus as the Christ. *Kairoi* are without doubt significant and momentous religious events, but they serve only as a preparation for the *kairos* which is unique. Jesus as the Christ is, for Tillich, the centre of the history of the manifestation of the Kingdom of God. He is the criterion by which all other manifestations are judged. Christianity is normative, therefore, in the sense that it bears witness to the *kairos*, the appearance of Jesus as the Christ.

The similarity is evident between Tillich's claim that the *kairoi* of religious history are a preparation for the *kairos*, the momentous event, of the advent of Jesus as the Christ, and the view of the Catholic theologians we have examined, for whom general sacred history and ordinary ways of salvation are a preparation for special sacred history and the extraordinary way of salvation revealed in Christ. The finality and normativeness of Christianity is emphasized in each case, and the justification Tillich offers for making this claim, as we have shown, is that it is an expression of the daring courage of the Christian faith, which without the risk of error would not be faith. It has to be acknowledged that this expression of faith, or religious judgement, does afford non-Christian religions a significant place in the religious history of mankind, and is an advance on the view that distinguishes between religion and faith and insists on the uniqueness of God's self-revelation in Christ to the exclusion of what is referred to as man's arrogant and futile attempts to come to know God by his own efforts. At least non-

Christian forms of revelation are on this view afforded a meaning and significance in the history of religion. Yet the point has to be made that it is difficult to see what is to prevent other religious traditions from making similar religious judgements based on what they consider to be the *kairos*, the momentous event of universal significance, or the extraordinary way of salvation, or special sacred history, within *their* traditions, and which for them would be an expression of the daring courage of *their* faith. The revelation of God in Christ may be normative and decisive for Christians and their ultimate criterion of truth, but what is to prevent different momentous events proving normative for followers of other religious traditions? If what we are confronted with is an expression of the daring courage of faith, and if the attempt to establish an independent criterion of truth to enable us to adjudicate between competing truth claims is mistaken and confused, then what we are left with is a choice between different religious judgements as to what is considered to be the final and normative revelation.

Such a claim to finality or normativeness, or what appears to be something close to it, is to be found in the work of one of the most significant reformers of modern India, namely, Vivekananda. Referred to by delegates attending the Parliament of Religions held in Chicago in 1893 as the 'cyclonic monk from India', Vivekananda travelled extensively in the cause of his spiritual mission. It was his unshakeable faith that India should conquer the world with her spirituality and it was this belief that motivated his efforts to arouse his fellow countrymen to the potency of their spiritual heritage. He travelled the length and breadth of India proclaiming his message that spirituality was the basis of the Hindu civilization and the fountain-head of social reform. Vedantic ideals, in his view, embodied this spirituality and if any religion could lay claim to be the universal religion then it had to be Advaita Vedanta.

> You hear claims made by every religion as being the universal religion of the world. Let me tell you in the first place that perhaps there will never be such a thing, but if there is a religion which can lay claim to be that, it is only our religion and no other, because every other religion depends on some person or persons.[7]

It is interesting to note that Vivekananda does not consider a religion based on the teachings of a historical person to be as strong and as satisfactory as one based on universal ideals. It is as if he is reluctant to link religion to the vagaries of historical investigations, for as he points out, 'disprove the historicity of the man and the whole fabric tumbles to the ground'.[8] As we have seen, Tillich was equally reluctant to submit the historical basis of Christianity to the vagaries and uncertainties of historical research, hence his attempt to provide Christianity with a fiducial guarantee for its own historical foundation.

What is it about the Vedantic religion then that makes it potentially of universal significance? That which is considered to be normative for the Christian religion, as we have indicated, is the person of Christ. For Vivekananda, however, the strength of Vedanta lies in its stress on the divinity of man or the presence of God in all men. The basic principle of Vedanta in his view is that all men have as their real nature the infinite ocean of *Sat Cit Ananda*, that is, Being, Consciousness, Bliss, which is *Brahman*.[9] There is but one life, one world, one existence, and the difference between one man and another is a difference of degree and not of kind. The same applies to the universe as a whole since God permeates all that exists from plants, stones, and animals to human beings.

> The difference between man and man, between angels and man, between man and animals, between animals and plants, between plants and stones is not in kind, because everyone from the highest angel to the lowest particle of matter is but an expression of that one infinite ocean, and the difference is only in degree. . . .You and I are both outlets of the same channel, and that is God; as such your nature is God, and so is mine. . . .The sum total of this whole universe is God Himself.[10]

Yet it is not enough that God be conceived of in personal terms alone. It is necessary to progress from the personal to the impersonal idea of God since the former is limited and the latter infinite. God is pure spirit; he is Truth – a sentiment which was to be echoed by Gandhi later. We need to seek God in the soul for 'He is the Soul. . . .When you think of Him as some one separate from yourself, you do not know Him. He is you yourself.'[11] The highest concept of God, according to Vivekananda, is the Vedantic concept of *Brahman*, that is, Being, Consciousness, Bliss, and constricting notions need to be superseded. The essence of religion is to see God as 'the Soul of our souls, the Reality in us'.[12] All that exists is in effect a manifestation of Being itself, which is the impersonal God. 'He is the essence of our own Self. He is the essence of this ego, thus I and we cannot know anything excepting in and through that I. Therefore you have to know everything in and through Brahman.'[13]

For Vivekananda, therefore, the impersonal God is the only reality; all else is unreal and manifested by the power of *maya* or illusion. Truth is *Brahman*, which is the Self of man, and the goal of life is to know the truth and attain to *Brahman*. We know *Brahman* when we know the truth that we are eternally one with the universal Being.[14]

While Vivekananda recognizes that for some the concept of a personal God may be necessary and has its rightful place, he regards it as an inferior position to adopt and a represention of a lower form of truth characteristic of the religion of the masses. In his view *dvaita*, dualism, is fulfilled by *visistadvaita*, qualified non-dualism, which in turn finds complete fulfilment in *advaita*, non-dualism.

> Now, as society exists at the present time, all these three stages are necessary; the one does not deny the other, one is simply the fulfilment of the other. The Advaitist or qualified Advaitist does not say that dualism is wrong; it is a right view, but a lower one. It is on the way to truth; therefore let everyone work out his own vision of this universe, according to his own ideas.[15]

It would appear then that the normative religion as far as Vivekananda is concerned is Advaita Vedanta. Dualistic concepts of religion are classified as 'on the way to truth'. This would apply to all forms of religion that conceive of God in personal terms and see man's ultimate goal as communion with God. On the face of it there seems little to distinguish this view from the exclusivism of the neo-orthodox position. Yet it has to be noted that while Vivekananda defines religion as in essence one and its goal as the realization of God in the soul, he recognizes that it takes different forms in accordance with the different circumstances in which people find themselves. He is careful to point out that as far as externals are concerned there are as many religions as there are human beings and that truth is capable of being expressed in a variety of different ways. This is a far cry from the point of view that would classify religion, as distinct from faith, as unbelief; yet it is very similar to the position that would regard 'other' religions as ordinary ways of salvation, or *kairoi*, which are in a sense preparatory, or to use Vivekananda's terminology, 'on the way to truth'. This is borne out by the distinction that is drawn between religion, or true spirituality, and religions; here, religion is considered to be synonymous with Advaita Vedanta and religions as preparatory paths to the realization of the goal of non-dualism. Vivekananda refers to them as grades of worship which struggle towards the real thing.[16] They are 'the little loves' which must be transcended before we arrive at our true goal which is the realization of God in the soul.[17] If we use the image of the tree, Advaita is the pinnacle and 'other' religions the lower branches, while the ladder image provides us with the picture of Advaita on the top rung and 'other' religions on the rungs beneath it. The similarity between this view and that of the liberal Catholic and Tillichian positions we have already referred to is evident.

In view of what Vivekananda has to say about Advaita Vedanta, we may ask whether what we have here is a religious judgement, or an expression of the daring courage of a particular form of the Hindu faith. If this confession of faith in the finality and normativeness of Advaita Vedanta stands in need of no external verification, then what we are left with is a choice between different religious judgements as to what is to be regarded as final and normative. Furthermore, on the basis of the religious judgement that Advaita Vedanta is the true goal of man's spiritual progress, is it not the case that Vedantists have the same right as members of other religious traditions to lead men by means of missionary activity to the realization of God in the soul?

ONE ESSENCE, MANY FORMS

An entirely opposite view to that taken by those who insist on the uniqueness, or the finality and normativeness of the Christian revelation is that which emphasizes the unitary nature of the essence, or transcendental form of religion. According to this view there may be different forms of religion but there is only one essence. The basic, underlying truth of religion is one, but it is possible to find many different historical forms of it. In the same way it might be said that there is but one religious goal for all mankind, but many paths to the realization of that goal. This is a view that unites the essentialist and relativist responses to religious pluralism and finds articulate expression in a number of different religious traditions.

As far as the Christian tradition is concerned we have seen that it finds expression in the theology of Schleiermacher, who conceives of religion as pre-existing all historical manifestations. Christianity, for him, is the most perfect and highly developed historical manifestation of the transcendental form of religion so far experienced by man, and the culmination of the progressive religious development of mankind. Yet other religions also, to a greater or lesser degree, manifest the essence or primordial form of religion, and to the degree that they do so, to that degree also they must be considered to be true. The possibility of further manifestations of the essence of religion cannot be ruled out, so it would appear to be inadvisable, from Schleiermacher's standpoint, to insist on the uniqueness and finality of the Christian revelation. This is in accordance with his view that religion originates in the soul's response to the universe, or what might also be called 'the sense and taste for the infinite', and so cannot be equated with any particular finite form. Different historical forms of religion are necessary, he claims, because people differ in their degree of apprehension and receptivity of the essence of religion, and it is for this very reason that religious pluralism is to be welcomed and the demand for uniformity must be rejected. Christianity may be distinctive, and the most highly developed form of religion that presently exists, yet it is not the only genuine historical form of religion possible. Different historical forms of religion are necessary in order that the one true essence of religion might be manifested, for without religious diversity, or religious pluralism, the primordial form of religion is not fully revealed. That is, the one transcendental essence requires many historical forms for its full and complete manifestation.

Hocking's reference to missionary activity as an attempt to make a particular religion universal, and his express desire to escape from activity of that kind, is an indication of his lack of enthusiasm for such a task. His antipathy to reducing the number of religions in the world by means of conversion to one so-called true religion is evident in his approval of the Chinese practice of supporting more than one religion. In this respect he is at one with Schleiermacher in supporting the need for religious pluralism, and in, implicity if not explicitly, pointing to the inadvisability of insisting on the uniqueness and finality of the Christian revelation. He advocates greater contact between members of different faiths in order that their religious experience might be broadened and their understanding of the essence of particular religions deepened. The reconception of a particular religion is part of the deepening process, for one's understanding of the essence of one's own religion can lead to a better grasp of the essence of all religions. This in turn is assisted by the broadening of one's religious experience through the mutual contact of members of different faiths. The ultimate goal for Hocking, therefore, is an understanding of the essence of all religions, and the broadening and deepening of one's understanding of particular religions is the means whereby this end can be achieved. The common ground between Hocking and Schleiermacher is evident. Both lay stress on the essence of religion and both approve of religious diversity. Hocking's reference to the possibility of a world faith deriving from the process of reconception does not mean, as it would appear at first sight, that he sees religious plurality giving way in due course to a single universal religion, but rather that he foresees a deeper understanding of particular religions emerging from mutual contact between members of different faiths. Like Schleiermacher, therefore, he advocates the view that the one transcendental essence of religion is in need of many historical forms for its complete manifestation.

For Otto the essence of religion is to be found in the concept of the holy which consists of both rational and non-rational elements. While both are essential for the understanding of religion it is the non-rational element of the numinous which lies at the heart of the idea of the holy and which is the essence of religion. It is the common ground of all religious consciousness. The influence of this view on those who have been concerned with religious plurality has been significant and it has had important implications for the study of religion. One of the conclusions that might be drawn from this phenomenological analysis of the common ground of religious consciousness, the non-rational element of the numinous, is that since it lies at the heart of all religions the difference between them is not one of essence but rather of form. If the idea of the holy is the essence of all religions then they differ from one another in degree and not in kind. It would appear that for Otto, as for those we have previously referred to, there is but one essence which expresses itself in many different forms.

The depth of the human psyche for Jung is the region of the collective unconscious in which archetypes or primordial images exist which are capable of serving as spiritual guides in man's life. One such archetype, or primordial image, is religiously expressed as God and psychologically as the Self, which points to the existence of a close correspondence between the soul and God. This is why it is psychologically unthinkable for God to be conceived as 'wholly other', in Jung's view, for such a conception would destroy the intimacy that exists between the soul and God. Religion is rooted in the human psyche and is not simply an outward form of faith consisting of creeds, dogmas, and rituals. The latter serve an important function nevertheless in the sense that they symbolize immediate experience, but they cannot be regarded as the embodiment of that experience in any way. As far as Jung is concerned the same applies to religions: they are all manifestations of the archetypes and as such are equally true. So it is not a question of one religion laying claim to uniqueness or finality to the exclusion or detriment of the others. The archetype of God or the Self might take the form of Christ, but it could also take the form of *Purusha* or *Atman* or *Hiranyagarbha* or the Buddha. What is suitable for some would be alien to others, hence the need of different religious forms to manifest the primordial images or archetypes.

So from his psychological starting point Jung arrives at the same conclusion as the essentialists we have already referred to, namely, that there are many forms of the primordial image or archetype of the Self or God. It would seem that Jung's archetypes, or primordial images, of the collective unconscious correspond to what is referred to in other contexts as the essence of religion, for religion, in his view, is rooted in the human psyche. But the primordial image or archetype is such that it cannot be expressed fully in any one particular religious form, and stands in need of many historical forms for its complete manifestation, all of which must be regarded as equally true.

From what Schleiermacher says about the need for the existence of different historical forms of religion in order that the essence of religion might be manifested, and from his rejection of demands for uniformity, we have to conclude that he is opposed to such missionary activity as would establish the existence of one historical religion to the exclusion of all others, and also to claims to uniqueness and finality made on behalf of a single historical religion. The same opposition appears in Hocking's work on the grounds that the mutual contact of members of different faiths leads to a better understanding of one's own religion as well as the essence of all religions. Such explicit views on mission are not to be found in the writings of either Otto or Jung, yet both claim that the essence of religion expresses itself in different historical forms, which differ from one another in degree and not in kind, and both hold that the different historical forms of religion are equally true.

Schleiermacher's reference to different historical forms of religion being necessary because people differ in their degree of apprehension and receptivity of the essence of religion is echoed in Toynbee's writings. Since God is love, he claims, then it is inconceivable that he should not reveal himself in accordance with man's ability to receive his revelation. To insist on the uniqueness and finality of the Christian revelation, therefore, is inappropriate and exclusivist claims must be relinquished if only because they are contrary to the idea of a loving, self-sacrificing God. For Toynbee then, as for the essentialists, the difference between the Christian revelation and divine revelation in other religions, is one of degree and not of kind. Like Hocking, he believes that respect and reverence for other faiths not only leads to a better understanding of one's own religion but also to a firmer grasp of the essence of all religions, and in this respect he claims to be echoing the views of Gandhi. God is the God of all mankind for Toynbee, and the light that shines through other faiths is derived from the same source as that which shines through Christ.

Troeltsch in his later writings finds it as difficult as Toynbee to uphold the absolute, exclusivist claims of Christianity. If, as he maintains, all things are subject to historical development including religious and ethical ideals, then there are difficulties involved in seeking to reconcile historical relativism with the claim of Christianity to embody the unique and final revelation. In Troeltsch's view there is an element of truth in all religions and because of this it is difficult to accept the claim of Christianity to be unique and normative, whether that claim is based on the traditional Church apologetic of supernatural revelation, or on the evolutionary apologetic of belief in Christianity as the fulfilment of the essence of religion. The notion of a progressive development from lower to higher forms of religious life culminating in Christianity is not borne out by the study of history. Neither is the naïvety of Christian apologetics concerning the normativeness of Christianity based on miracles sustainable from the standpoint of historical investigation. The more the historical character of Christianity is recognized, the greater is the tendency for claims to uniqueness and absolute truth to retreat into the background.

Christianity is true and normative for Christians, according to Troeltsch, but not necessarily for all people. The point Troeltsch is making is that the Christian may make a religious judgement concerning the normativeness of Christianity for himself, based on his personal convictions, but he has to allow that similar judgements may be made by adherents of other religious traditions, based on their own personal convictions. Hinduism and Buddhism may be normative and true for adherents of those faiths, for example, in exactly the same way Christianity is for Christians. The concept of conversion from one religion to another, therefore, by means of missionary activity must give way to the quest for mutual understanding. Here Troeltsch reflects the views of Schleirmacher, Hocking, and Toynbee, and it is his belief that mutual understanding is achieved when each religion realizes its own potential, yet remains open to the influence of other religions in their quest for truth. What has to be acknowledged, he claims, is that there are many different experiences of the Divine, determined in no small measure by the cultural and social milieu in which they are encountered.

We have suggested that the essentialist response to religious pluralism finds expression in a number of different religious traditions and the same may be true of the relativist response which we have noted in our analysis of the positions of Troeltsch and Toynbee. An example of the essentialist response is to be found in the Hindu tradition in the works of Radhakrishnan and Gandhi. The former agrees with Schleiermacher that the predominant element in the religious consciousness is feeling, which is distinct from creaturely feeling and also the Kantian concept of moral consciousness, and has within it a sense of the mystical. As far as Hinduism is concerned, Radhakrishnan is of the view that it affirms the significance of the life of the spirit and he sees the aim of the Hindu way of life as coming to know and possess this spirit.[18] Futhermore he refers to it as 'a movement not a position; a process not a result; a growing tradition not a fixed revelation'.[19] For Radhakrishnan, there is no discontinuity between human life and spiritual life or between animal life and human life. All forms of life are expressions of the Divine Spirit, for the whole world is a manifestation of God or the Spirit.

On the question of the encounter of different religions he recognizes the importance of learning about the basic principles of the great religions of the world and sees it as essential to the promotion of international understanding. No world community or culture is possible where inter-religious rivalries prevail, and the promotion of inter-religious understanding involves the abandonment of missionary activity and prosyletising, which presupposes the belief that one religion is in some way superior to another. No single religion, in Radhakrishnan's view, can lay claim to exclusivity. All religious traditions are imperfect expressions of the immutable essence of religion that is ultimate truth. Claims to finality are responsible for intolerance and fanaticism and aggressive attitudes towards other forms of life. Like Toynbee and Troeltsch, Radhakrishnan maintains that we need to abandon such claims.

> If we look upon our dogmatic formulations as approximations to the truth and not the truth itself, then we must be prepared to modify them if we find other propositions which enter deeper into reality. On such a view it will be illogical for us to hold that any system of theology is an official, orthodox, obligatory and final presentation of the truth.[20]

All historical traditions are partial and defective, in Radhakrishnan's view, and we need to recognize that fact and 'seek their source in the generic tradition from which they have all sprung'.[21]

That there are many expressions of the one ultimate truth seems to be at the heart of Radhakrishnan's philosophy, and although religious truth may be seen in different ways by different religions it is still the case that truth is ultimately one. 'Every expression of truth is relative. It cannot possess an unique value to the exclusion of others. It cannot be the only possible expression of what it expresses.'[22]

A similar response to religious pluralism is to be found in the writings of Gandhi. His concept of religion corresponds to his concept of truth. As he glimpses absolute truth through particular, relative instances of truth so he glimpses religion, or the essence of religion, through particular, historical religions. For what he means by religion, as he indicates, is that which underlies all religions: that which transcends them, yet harmonizes them and gives them reality.[23] It is not possible for a particular, historical religion to embody the perfection of religion or to lay claim to a monopoly of the truth. Exclusivist claims must be rejected. Religions are imperfect human constructs or expressions of that which underlies them and gives them reality. The heart of one religion is at one with the heart of another religion. 'Even as a tree has a single trunk, but many branches and leaves, so there is one true and perfect religion, but it becomes many, as it passes through the human medium.'[24]

If Gandhi is referring to the essence or primordial form of religion when he speaks of the heart of one religion being at one with the heart of another, then it may be possible to point to similarities between his position and that of Schleiermacher and the other essentialists we have referred to. What is abundantly clear, however, is that, for Gandhi, as for Vivekananda, all religions are different paths to the same goal and that there will always be a variety of religions corresponding to different human temperaments and cultural environments.[25] And given the imperfect nature of all particular religons, it follows that missionary activity and conversion from one religion to another ought to give way to mutual understanding.[26] In this respect Gandhi echoes Troeltsch and as we have seen he also inspired Toynbee when he maintained that his study of other religions enabled him to acquire a better understanding of his own faith.[27]

It will be clear that the essentialist and relativist responses to religious pluralism do not favour apologetics or any form of exclusivism. Claims to uniqueness and finality, and attempts to convert from one religion to another through missionary activity, are rejected. If the essence of religion is one, and if all historical forms of religion are relative, then it makes no sense for one particular historical form or expression of religion to lay claim to a monopoly of the truth. We have seen that the essentialist view presupposes the existence of a transcendental essence or primordial form of religion. The question is whether such a transcendental essence is capable of being isolated and how we would recognize it in the event of it being isolated. Is Cantwell Smith right to maintain that the attempt to seek the essence of religion detracts from a true understanding of particular historical religions? And is it possible to take that point further by claiming that without the existence of particular historical religions it would not be possible to conceive of an essence of religion in the first place? Again is Troeltsch correct when he claims that historical investigation reveals no universal principle underlying particular religions? And is Kung right to insist that to speak of an essence of religion underlying all particular forms and expressions is as much an affirmation of faith as the claim that Christianity is the unique, final, and normative religion for all mankind? Is it the case that what we have here is simply a religious or perhaps a metaphysical judgement, and an affirmation of the daring courage of the essentialist faith?

THE NEED FOR DIALOGUE

It was perhaps inevitable that the dialogical approach to religious pluralism should have found favour in recent years if only because of the close encounter of the faiths of different peoples of the world as a result of the development of what has come to be known as the global village. Among the characteristics of the dialogical approach from the standpoint of Christianity has been a reassessment and reinterpretation of the doctrine of the incarnation. In place of the view that stresses the divinity of Christ as the second person of the Trinity, is that which recognizes the mythological character of much of the Church's teaching concerning the incarnation, and favours instead emphasis on the humanity of Jesus. This finds expression in Hick's advocacy of a Copernican revolution in theology whereby Christocentricity gives way to theocentricity – which has important implications for the encounter of Christianity with other world religions. Like Troeltsch, he endeavours to preserve the concept of general revelation in the context of different cultural traditions, and seeks to show that it is only right and proper to believe that God has revealed himself through other religious traditions in addition to Christianity. What this means is that, for Hick, claims made for the uniqueness of the Christian faith are inappropriate. The Christian encounter with God does not preclude the possibility of other encounters beyond the boundaries of Christianity. Christian claims to exclusivity are dangerously dogmatic and in any event impossible to support. Other world faiths provide ways of salvation for men which are not automatically rendered null and void by the Christian claim to uniqueness and finality. Christianity stands in need of dialogue in order that God might be seen to be at work in the whole religious life of mankind.

Smart's view, which preceded that of Hick, also favours dialogue, the rules of which are evaded by the apologetic approach. He deplores the myopia of modern theology on the question of general revelation and supports the view that there are many revelations. It follows that the relation of the great religions of the world to one another cannot be avoided, and that it is not possible for one particular religion to lay claim to universal validity. Not only are different faiths likely to continue, according to Smart, but so also are different models or forms of the same faith. Since this is the case the pluralistic solution makes sense. Given that there are many revelations, many different types of religious experience, many different strands of religious discourse, and many different goals of truth, it follows that, for Smart, no serious student of religion can possibly afford to ignore the comparative study of religion. Hence the need for dialogue, which unfortunately the confessional, apologetic, and traditionally theological approach to religious pluralism tends to ignore. The tendency of the confessional approach, as we suggested earlier, is to provide 'comparative' religion with a minor role in the theological curriculum; this leads, as we have seen, to the development of a ghetto mentality which confines theologians to their own religious traditions in isolation from the spiritual insights of other faiths.

Cantwell Smith's personal dialogical approach further underlies the fact that we need to understand religious traditions other than our own if we are to avoid cultivating a ghetto mentality. For him, as for other supporters of dialogue, exclusivism is unacceptable, displaying as it does human arrogance and an implicit denial of the love of God. He favours a world community with a world theology and sees no possiblity of that kind of community being established if the confessional, apologetic, and prosyletising mood prevails within particular religions. His emphasis is on understanding religions from within, although, as we have seen, he prefers the term faith to religion. It may be that his attempt to move towards the establishment of a world theology can be viewed as utopian in the sense that it fails to take into account or acknowledge the distinctive nature of particular forms of life, but that does not detract from the importance of his contribution to the dialogical approach to religious pluralism. His explicit reference to the arrogance of exclusivism means that he would hardly take kindly to Rahner's reference to 'anonymous' Christians. Given his views concerning the dangers of circumscribing the love of God, it is also unlikely that he would approve of the distinctions drawn by Schlette and Kung between general and sacred history and between ordinary and extraordinary ways of salvation.

Like Smith, Panikkar favours seeing the truth from within more than one religious tradition and considers it to be the means of a renewal of faith. The purpose of intra-religious dialogue, however, is not conversion, or the creation of a single universal religion, but the promotion of mutual understanding. He is at one with other supporters of the dialogical approach in totally rejecting apologetics and claims to exclusivism, and in recognizing the significance of the historical dimension and the cultural and social milieu in the formulation of different religious traditions. The principle of homogeneity has to be accepted, in Panikkar's view, that is, seeking to understand particular religions from within their religio-cultural contexts, but the principle of dialogue has also to be accepted if we are to make progress towards mutual understanding. Intra-religious dialogue must be succeeded by inter-religious dialogue, which has to be authentic in the sense that we have to accept that it might lead to *metanoia*, or a complete change in our own religious outlook. Here Panikkar goes much further than other supporters of the dialogical approach. He accepts the possible consequences of genuine dialogue, namely, that one might be so convinced of the truth of a position as to be prepared to relinquish the position previously held in favour of one which provides what is considered to be a better understanding of the truth. As we have seen, Panikkar believes fervently in the existential nature and universal validity of truth. But truth takes many forms, such as Christ, Vishnu, Rama, or Krishna, and the divine mystery might be expressed in the form of the Trinity or Advaita Vedanta. So we need to recognize that that which is the goal of the religious experience of mankind allows for a variety of approaches. That is, we need to adopt a positive attitude to religious pluralism.

The dialogical approach to the study of religion that Tillich embarked upon towards the end of his life owes much, as we have seen, to his personal encounter with representatives of Japanese religions. But his theological training had already shown him the dangers of exclusivism and biblical narrowness and the need for a deeper understanding of the nature of the holy. His analysis of the nature of the holy as the universal ground of religion, and his view that the constituent elements of the holy are the sacramental, mystical, and prophetic, provides him with the means for engaging in intra-religious and inter-religious dialogue. While his attempt to show how dialogue can take place between Buddhism and Christianity, based on the type-determining elements of the holy, reveal certain shortcomings, there is no doubt that he succeeds in showing how inter-religious dialogue can promote greater understanding between religions. Like other supporters of the dialogical approach he rejects exclusivism and favours the view that revelation is universal and appropriated by man in the context of his cultural tradition. Earlier in his theological career, however, as we have seen, he distinguishes between preparatory and final revelation, indicating that *kairoi* of religious history are a preparation for, and subject to the judgement of, the *kairos* of Jesus as the Christ. The justification he offers for making this claim is that it is an expression of the daring courage of the Christian faith. We have already commented on the problems related to this particular view, but what is important to note in this context is that non-Christian forms of revelation are afforded a significant if subordinate place in Tillich's view of the history of religions. It has to be admitted, however, that if his preparatory-final revelatory distinction determines his approach to inter-religious dialogue then it can hardly be said to be open-ended. It is far removed from Panikkar's more positive approach to the plurality of religions which allows for the possibility of *metanoia*. And from the standpoint also of other supporters of the dialogical approach it might be seen as favouring the confessional, apologetic approach. Is it possible that as we distinguish between the earlier and later Wittgenstein so we need to distinguish between the earlier and later Tillich?

The dialogical approach to religious puralism finds expression in different religious traditions in the same way as does the essentialist response. The basic prerequisites of dialogue are to be found in the writings of the eloquent and enthusiastic Keshub Chunder Sen, who was initiated into the Brahmo Samaj by Devendranath Tagore. This was a society founded by Rammohan Roy in 1828 to promote a lofty theism and to restore religious purity within Hinduism. Sen's view on religions is that they do not embody absolute truth yet neither are they absolutely false, and he maintains that:

> We must not, therefore, pronounce indiscriminate condemnation upon any creed, nor cherish sectarian antipathy towards its followers. We should distinguish what is true in them from its false administers, and in a liberal spirit note the power features common to all creeds.[28]

The same prerequisites for dialogue are to be found in the teaching of the mystic Ramakrishna who exercised a powerful influence on a dedicated group of disciples, of whom Vivekananda was the most prominent, and which included Sen. For Ramakrishna all religions are true and worthy of respect. He maintains,

> It is not good to feel that one's religion alone is true and all others are false. God is one only and not two. Different people call him by different names. . . . Each religion is only a path leading to God, as rivers come from different directions and ultimately become one in the one ocean.[29]

As we have seen, the equality of religions finds eloquent expression in the teaching of Gandhi. All religions, for him, are rivers flowing to the same ocean or branches of the same tree. His readiness to acknowledge that God is all things to all men enables him to maintain that it makes no difference whether a devotee conceives of God in personal or impersonal terms. His acceptance of the Jain doctrine of *anekantavada*, or the doctrine of the manyness of reality, by which is meant that reality can be conceived of in many different ways, depending on the point of view that is adopted, makes it possible for him to approve of the non-creative aspect of God propounded by the Jains, the creative aspect of God as propounded by Ramanuja, as well as maintaining his own preference for *advaita* or non-Dualism. That this tolerant attitude should have resulted in his being referred to as an *anekantavadin* is perfectly understandable and did not disturb him in the least. In fact he might well have considered it a compliment, since he believed that *anekantavada* was one of the most significant doctrines he had learnt from Jainism.[30] It was this doctrine that enabled him to implement the dialogical principle in the way keenly favoured by Cantwell Smith, namely, to view religions, or the faiths of other men, empathetically from within. 'I very much like this doctrine of the manyness of reality. It is this doctrine that has taught me to judge a Mussalman from his own standpoint and a Christian from his.'[31] When his attitude of toleration is combined with respect for all religions and belief in their equality, what we have in effect in Gandhi is a combination of the essentialist response to religious pluralism with a recognition of the need for dialogue.[32]

THE COSMIC CHRIST

The response to religious pluralism that conceives of the concept of the transcendent Christ being applied to religions other than Christianity bears the hallmark of the neo-orthodox approach that stresses the uniqueness of the Christian faith. M. M. Thomas's acknowledgement of his indebtedness to Barth, and his attempt to unveil the significance of Christ in the faiths of other men, is an implicit recognition of the similarities between his view and that of the neo-orthodox theologians. He appears to go further than the theologians mentioned, however, when he makes the point that he does not wish to regard classical Christologies as binding, and seeks to encourage the use of non-Christian categories to reveal the uniqueness of Christ. When he maintains that the dynamics of salvation may be discerned in the Asian renaissance, and makes mention of Gandhi's reference to Jesus as the supreme *satyagrahi*, he seems to be suggesting that Hindu categories might be used to reveal *The Acknowledged Christ of the Indian Renaissance* which, as we have shown, is the title of his book. More humanistic categories seem to apply, however, when it is maintained that men are responding to Jesus as the Christ when they acknowledge that human existence is grounded in love. This existentialist response on Thomas's part, which reflects his concern to promote authentic human existence, takes him beyond the traditional categories that would apply in both the Christian and Hindu religious traditions. Whether he becomes aware of this humanistic trend or not, he hastens to assure us that the attempt to discern the redemptive work of Christ outside the Church ought not be taken to imply that the love ethic, or a mystical experience, is an adequate substitute for the Gospel. His minimal flirtation with mild forms of existentialism and humanism does not really affect his adherence to the concept of the uniqueness of the transcendental Christ.

The cosmic, transcendental Christ is as normative for Devanandan as it is for Thomas, and, in his view, is capable of being manifested in the demand for justice and the desire to create a new humanity. This is characteristic of all religions and not only Christianity. The parallels that might be drawn between this view and the traditional Logos doctrine is evident. It is as if the transcendental Christ corresponds to the Logos, which was in the beginning, which was made flesh, and which is the light that lightens every man that comes into the world.

Samartha makes specific use of non-Christian categories to reveal the uniqueness of Christ when he seeks to formulate a Christology that would be in accordance with Indian thought forms. The unbound, unlimited Christ is universal, he claims, and cannot be confined to Christianity. He might be described within the Hindu tradition as the great *advaitin*, or the ideal *satyagrahi*, or one of the many *avatara* of the Divine. Or he might be regarded as a guru to be followed rather than a God to be worshipped, and his saving work might be interpreted in *advaitin* terms as liberation from the bondage of *samsara* with its egocentricity, and its concept of the world as *maya* or illusion. For Samartha, the real possibility for the formulation of an Indian Christology lies with *advaita*. The immanence of the Hindu tradition, he claims, might be fruitfully balanced by the transcendence of the Christian tradition and vice versa. Similarly the historicity of one tradition might be complemented by the stress on the unity of life in the other tradition. But the whole purpose behind the formulation of an Indian Christology, and the attempt to manifest the cosmic Christ in the religious and social life of India, is to reveal the uniqueness of the revelation of God in Christ. In this respect there is little to distinguish the Christocentric approach of these writers from the neo-orthodox response to religious pluralism that we have already examined. The same questions that were raised in connection with that response apply in this context. If what we have here is a confession of faith, or a religious judgement, then there would appear to be nothing to prevent adherents of other religious traditions from making similar confessions of faith and making similar claims to uniqueness for the revelation of God within their traditions. This would appear to be one of the crucial issues for discussion in any attempt to construct a theology of religions.

Chapter Eleven

CONCLUSION

Our analysis and assessment of the different responses to religious pluralism has clarified some of the main issues that would have to be dealt with if we would seek to formulate a theology of religions. If we were content with a purely phenomenological approach to religious plurality then it might conceivably be possible for us to assume the role of neutral observers in our approach to world religions. But there are problems involved in seeking to adopt a neutralist position. Since we are all culturally and socially determined, and existentially bound to particular forms of life, it is difficult to see how we can be totally neutral even if we were to adopt a purely phenomenological approach to religious pluralism. Theological responses, however, are of a different order and it would appear that certain presuppositions are unavoidable on this level.

What has clearly emerged from our examination hitherto is that it is no longer possible for the conscientious theologian to ignore the existence of different religious traditions. There may still be a tendency in some quarters to assign 'comparative' religions a subordinate place in the theological curriculum, but there can be no doubt that the theological education of any student who is denied access to the religious and spiritual insights of religious traditions other than his own will be severely limited and sadly circumscribed. The point is well made that no serious student of religion can really afford to ignore the study of comparative religion. This is well illustrated in the experience of Tillich whose theological outlook seemed to undergo both a broadening and a deepening, or a reconception as Hocking would say, following his encounter with Buddhist and Shinto priests in Japan. The importance he attached to the study of comparative religion from that moment on did not mean, of course, that he considered the traditional forms of theological study to be irrelevant in comparison. It meant rather that, in his view, theological investigation had to be conducted in the wider context of the spiritual insights of world religions if it were to be considered relevant, and his suggestion is that it would benefit greatly from being pursued in this way.

One of the significant issues relating to our examination of the responses to religious pluralism is the concept of uniqueness. We have seen that, as far as Christianity is concerned, it raises the question of the uniqueness of the revelation of God in Christ. The implication of the exclusivist view concerning the uniqueness of God's self-disclosure is that all other claims to revelation must of necessity be regarded as either inadequate or imperfect. This confessional view provides ample justification for the apologetic approach and for missionary activity, because it can be maintained that it is incumbent upon recipients of the unique revelation of God to share it with those who have not been so favourably blessed. That is, it might be considered the natural consequence of believing that we have received the fullness of the revelation of God that we should wish to share it with others, and that such a belief demands apologetics. The problem arises when what is ostensibly a confession of faith comes to be regarded as a statement of fact which cannot be questioned. The consequence of equating a religious judgement, or a confession of faith, with a statement of fact in this fashion is that similar claims made by adherents of other religious traditions in their turn to be the recipients of the fullness of God's revelation are not considered to be true.

We have suggested that the search for an external criterion of truth whereby we might adjudicate between competing truth claims is both confused and mistaken. If it is maintained, contrary to this view, that the truth of Christianity can be verified eschatologically in the lives of believing Christians, then it would follow that it must be possible for the same eschatological verification to apply in the lives of believing Hindus concerning the truth of Hinduism. Yet if religious truths are held to be self-evident then it makes little sense to talk of those truths being verified eschatologically in the lives of religious believers.

Again it might be maintained that morality could be regarded as an external criterion of truth since immoral actions can belie our confession of faith, thereby proving our religious beliefs to be misguided or false. But the fact is that morality is not something which is independent of a particular form of life. We learn what is right and wrong within a form of life rather than as neutral observers. The same principle applies to the attempt to make religious experience an external criterion of truth. The fact is that religious experience occurs within religious traditions; it is difficult to conceive of it having a life of its own independent of particular, historical religions.

If we were to refer to God's self-disclosure in Christ as an objective, independent criterion of truth in itself, we might be considered guilty of confusing a confession of faith with a statement of fact. In the same way the attempt to make the mystical experience of the essence, or transcendental unity, of religion an independent criterion of truth is equally confused, for, as we have seen, it is as much a confession of faith as the claim that God has revealed himself in Christ. The impersonal mystical approach is as dogmatic in its own way as the more personal approach of neo-orthodoxy. Furthermore the question as to how we would isolate and apprehend the primordial form, or transcendental unity, of religion remains. From what we have said it will be evident that the danger of confusing a confession of faith with a statement of fact is a very real one. There may well be grounds for adjudicating between religions when it comes to the question of consistency, factual correctness, or correspondence with what we know to be true in other circumstances, but as far as truth claims are concerned there are no criteria independent of the religious traditions concerned to which we can appeal, and attempts to establish such criteria are mistaken and confused. We have to concede, therefore, that there are different religions and different moralities grounded in different forms of life.

What we have to conclude from our examination is that it is not possible for the claim to uniqueness to be confined to the Christian tradition. Confessions of faith are characteristic of all religious traditions and we have to accept the fact that there is nothing to prevent followers of other religions from making a similar claim to uniqueness as that to be found in Christianity. Representations made on behalf of the Vedic faith within the Hindu tradition is a case in point and could be matched by other examples.

Furthermore, it is as well to recognize that the role played by the social and cultural milieu in which we are nurtured in determining our religious attitudes is both significant and important, for without a doubt metaphysical beliefs acquired within a particular form of life tend to inform our outlook and determine the spirit in which we live our lives.

It is clear that the claim to uniqueness made on behalf of a historical, religious tradition has a major role to play in any attempt to formulate a theology of religions. If it is upheld, then it points automatically to the superiority of that particular religious tradition. No distinction that might be drawn between faith or revelation and religion can alter that fact. It may be argued in the case of Christianity that as a religion it is as much under the judgement of the self-revelation of God in Christ as all other religions, but the fact remains that its witness to that revelation is what is believed to make it superior to all other religions. The kind of theology of religions that is likely to emerge from maintaining this concept of uniqueness, as we have seen, is one that assigns other religions to the realm of unbelief or man's futile attempts to know God. So if it were to be acknowledged that a genuine awareness of the divine occurs in all religious traditions, and that the love of God in Christ is not incompatible with the love of God expressed in other forms and under other circumstances, a theology of religions based on the exclusive claims to uniqueness made on behalf of a particular religious tradition would have to be regarded as unacceptable.

A further significant issue that emerges from our examination of the different responses to religious pluralism and that has to be addressed in any attempt to formulate a theology of religions is that which distinguishes between preparatory and final revelation. It is a modification of the claim to uniqueness in that it allows for the possibility of universal revelation. On this view at least man is not groping about in the darkness of unbelief, or making futile attempts to know God by his own efforts. It is acknowledged that God reveals himself in many different ways, yet an element of exclusiveness is retained when it is insisted that the final or normative revelation by which all other revelations are to be judged, is to be found in God's self-disclosure in Christ. It makes little difference ultimately whether the stated distinction takes the form of preparatory and final revelation, or general and special sacred history, or ordinary and extraordinary ways of salvation, or *kairoi* and *kairos*; the principle remains the same. As with the uniqueness claim, on this view also the fullness of truth is located in Christ and the desire to share this knowledge with others remains the same. The apologetic approach is as much the hallmark of this modified view as it is of exclusivism. But since what we have here is a confession of faith rather than a statement of fact, there would seem to be nothing to prevent adherents of religious traditions other than Christianity from making similar claims to finality or normativeness. This is precisely what has been done, as we have seen, and it would seem to be natural for them also to wish to share their knowledge with others. That is, the apologetic approach is as much an integral part of claims to finality and normativeness as it is of claims to uniqueness irrespective of the religious traditions in which such claims are made.

The claim to finality has important implication for any attempt to formulate a theology of religions. If such a view is upheld then the particular religion for which finality is claimed must be regarded as distinctive and in many ways superior to other religions. The distinction between preparatory and final revelation may not be regarded as a distinction between faith and religion as with the exclusivist position, but it is just as significant. On the assumption that the love of God is universal and that it does not differ in kind from one form of religion to another, then a theology of religions based on the concept of the final and normative revelation finding expression in a particular religious tradition would appear to be unacceptable.

Another significant issue that emerges from our examination of the responses to religious pluralism relates to the concept of an essence of religion pre-existing historical forms of religion. The point has been made that belief in a primordial form, or transcendental unity, of religion as the a priori condition of all particular historical forms, is as much a confession of faith as claims to uniqueness or finality made on behalf of particular religions. But as a confession of faith that regards all historical religions as concrete expressions of a primordial form of religion, and true in so far as they succeed in expressing the primordial form, the essentialist view cannot, or at least ought not to, make claims to uniqueness or finality on behalf of particular religions. It is interesting to note, however, that as far as Schleiermacher is concerned, a claim for finality or distinctiveness, though not uniqueness, seems to be made on behalf of the Christian faith. Even so he does not want it to be regarded as a universal religion, or the only genuine form of religion. The revelation of God is available through other forms, albeit to a lesser degree, and they are in fact essential for the complete manifestation of the essence of religion. This is the reason why Hocking in his turn sees no reason to reduce the number of religions in the world for, in his view, mutual contact between religions leads to deeper self-understanding. The implication of this view is that apologetics and missionary activity leading to conversion from one religion to another are not favoured, and despite his emphasis on the distinctiveness of Christianity, Schleiermacher insists that the divine can be discerned in a variety of different ways and that religious uniformity is unacceptable. Christian piety, in his view, is just one form of piety among many, and religious diversity and multiplicity is essential for the manifestation of the transcendental unity of religion.

It will be seen that the essentialist response is a more liberal approach than that which would insist on the uniqueness or finality of a particular, religious tradition. It certainly does not seek to make a particular religion universal, nor does it favour apologetics. This is borne out by Otto. If the numinous lies at the heart of all religions, as he claims, and if it is the common ground of religious consciousness, then all religions have a part to play in the development of the spiritual life of mankind. The Buddha symbol has as significant a role to play in the religious life of man as the Christ symbol, which is why, according to Jung, no religion can lay claim to uniqueness or finality.

The problem with the essentialist view, however, as Troeltsch points out, is that historical investigation can point to no universal principle underlying particular, historical manifestations of religion. References to an essence of religion, therefore, cannot look to historical investigation for ratification. But since what we have here is a confession of faith rather than a statement of fact, we would hardly expect it to be ratified by historical research. Neither would we expect to be able to isolate the essence of religion in the same way as we would isolate aspects of particlar religions. A further problem with the essentialist approach is that opponents might argue that far from the primordial form of religion pre-existing particular forms of religion, the essence of religion might be understood only from our knowledge and understanding of particular, religious traditions.

Despite these reservations, however, it would seem that the essentialist view offers a better prospect of formulating an acceptable theology of religions than the exclusivist or normative views we have outlined. At least it offers all religions a significant role in the development of the spiritual life of mankind. The same might be said of the relativist response to religious pluralism, according to which particular forms of religions are considered to be different manifestations of the divine in history. The historical approach, so characteristic of the relativist reponse to religious plurality, makes it difficult if not impossible for any particular religion to lay claim to uniqueness or normativeness. Neither is it possible from the historical standpoint to speak of a progressive development from lower to higher forms of life culminating for some in Christianity. The Christian faith may be the highest form of truth for the Christian, but it does not necessarily follow that it is the highest form of truth for followers of other religions. The point is that it cannot claim to be *the* universal religion.

It is clear that the relativist response has important implications for the concept of mission. It recognizes that our concern must be for mutual understanding rather than conversion from one religion to another. Each religion has to realize its own potential and at the same time it has to be recognized that our experience of the divine is not one but many. From the standpoint of relativism, therefore, any attempt to formulate a theology of religions has to acknowledge religious plurality as a fact of existence. It is not possible to make an objective assessment of the value of different religions since proofs of value are derived from within particular cultures which determine the development of religions in the first place. That is, there is no external criterion of truth to enable us to distinguish between the value and validity of different truth claims.

The similarity between what we have referred to as the Christocentric response to religious pluralism and the exclusivist approach is such that the same conclusions can be drawn in each case. What is distinctive about this response is that here exclusivity takes the form of unveiling the significance of the cosmic, transcendental Christ in the teaching of all religions and not only Christianity. To use traditional Christian terminology, it might be claimed that while the eternal Logos was made flesh in Christ, and in that form is effective for man's salvation through the Christian tradition, its saving power is nevertheless universal and effective in all religious traditions. That is, the unbound, unlimited Christ, the eternal Logos, cannot be confined to one religious tradition.

The same problems that applied to the exclusivist approach apply equally to the Christocentric response. If it is accepted that a genuine awareness of the divine mystery occurs in all religious traditions and that the love of God is universal, no theology of religions that would seek to circumscribe the love of God, or undermine and belittle man's awareness of God in religious traditions other than Christianity, could possibly be regarded as acceptable.

The dialogical response to religious pluralism is one that has found favour in recent years. This is perhaps not surprising given that the world has contracted in size because of the speed of modern travel and the excellence of moderm communications. Among the issues that emerge from a more open-ended dialogical approach to religious plurality is the need for a reassessment of the significance of religious traditions other than one's own and a recognition of the need to understand them empathetically from within. Panikkar speaks of the need to accept the principle of homogeneity, by which he means that religious concepts can only be properly understood empathetically from within the particular religious traditions in which they occur. An important aspect of the empathetic approach also, as Cantwell Smith points out, is that we come to realize that we are dealing with real people and not just with systems and institutions. Dialogue is facilitated when it is conducted on a personal footing and when it is acknowledged that we are dealing with the faith of other men. Open-endedness in dialogue, therefore, involves the total rejection of exclusivism with its apologetic and proselytizing attitude, which might be regarded as a form of arrogance and presumptiousness and an attempt to limit the love of God. It enables us to recognize that the divine mystery, or the concept of transcendence, or the concept of truth, which in Christianity takes the form of the revelation of God in the person of Christ, might take other forms in other religious traditions.

A possible consequence of the dialogical approach is that it might lead us to acknowledge that there are different religions and different moralities grounded in different forms of life, and to accept the fact that religious pluralism makes a significant contribution towards the growth and development of world civilizations. It might also enable us to recognize that the different religions of the world complement one another and serve to enlarge our vision of the transcendent, enhance the richness of our spiritual experience, and deepen our understanding of the truth. Recognition of the fact that the divine mystery can take different forms in different religious traditions might also prompt the question why uniformity should be considered so desirable, and whether complementarity is not preferable to exclusivity.

Another issue that emerges from the dialogical response, as far as Christianity is concerned, is the need for a reinterpretation of the traditional doctrine of the person of Christ with which the concept of exclusiveness is associated. As a notable representative of the dialogical approach Hick insists on the mythological character of much of the Church's teaching on the subject of the incarnation and stresses the importance of the humanity of Jesus. When the traditional Christocentric response to religious pluralism gives way to the theocentric approach, 'other' religions assume greater significance and the concept of general revelation comes to the fore. Claims to exclusiveness and finality are also rejected in favour of dialogue. And when dialogue is truly authentic and open-ended it can involve those concerned with it in *metanoia*, or a complete change of religious outlook. There is no question of bracketing one's own faith while engaging in dialogue, and representatives of this approach, like Panikkar, acknowledge that truth takes many forms and that we need to pursue the goal of truth wherever it may lead us. For all representatives of this response to religious pluralism, however, dialogue is seen as an implicit recognition that there are many revelations, many different types of religious experience, many different strands of religious discourse, and many different forms of truth. It might, therefore, be regarded as an acceptable response to religious pluralism.

NOTES

1 CONCERN WITH PLURALITY

1 Don Wiebe, 'A Positive Episteme for the Study of Religion', *The Scottish Journal of Religious Studies*, vol.VI 2, (Autumn 1985), p. 91

2 Joseph M. Kitagawa, 'The History of Religions in America', *The History of Religions: Essays in Methodology*, ed. by Mircea Eliade and Joseph M. Kitagawa (Chicago: University of Chicago Press, 1959), p.15

3 Ibid., pp. 18, 21

4 Ibid., p. 19

5 Wilfred Cantwell Smith, 'Comparative Religion: Whither – and Why?', *The History of Religion: Essays in Methodology* (Chicago: Uversity of Chicago Press, 1959), p. 55

6 Rudolph Otto, *The Idea of the Holy* (New York: Oxford University Press, 1958), pp. 4, 8

7 J. M. Kitagawa, 'The History of Religions in America', pp. 5–7; cf. Ninian Smart, *The Science of Religion and the Sociology of Knowledge* (Princeton: Princeton University Press, 1973), chap. I

8 Wilfred Cantwell Smith, 'Comparative Religion: Whither – and Why?', pp. 34–5

9 Ibid., p. 42

10 Ibid., pp. 44, 47, 49

11 Ibid., p. 54

12 Ibid., p. 55

13 W. Cantwell Smith, *Towards a World Theology* (London: Macmillan, 1981), p. 152

14 Ibid., p. 168

15 Don Wiebe, 'A Positive Episteme for the Study of Religion', pp.85–7

16 W. Cantwell Smith, *The Meaning and End of Religion* (New York: Mentor, 1964), p. 46 and p. 232nn., pp. 40, 54

17 Cf. H. B. Acton, 'Georg Wilhelm Friedrich Hegel', in *The Encyclopedia of Philosophy*, vols 3, 4 (New York: Macmillan, 1967); Bertrand Russell, *A History of Western Philosophy* (London: George Allen & Unwin, 1946) pp. 757–61; John Macquarrie, *20th Century Religious Thought* (London: SCM Press 1963), pp. 23–4

18 Friedrich Schleiermacher, *On Religion: Speeches to its Cultured Despisers* (New York: Harper, 1958), pp. 40, 54
19 Ibid., pp. 236, 238
20 *The Meaning and End of Religion*, p. 21
21 Ibid., pp. 48, 55
22 Ibid., pp. 114, 134
23 Ibid., p. 135
24 Ibid., pp. 141, 162, 175
25 *Vatican Council II: the Conciliar and Post Conciliar Documents*, general editor Austin Flannery (New York: Costello Publishing Company, 1975, 1984), vol. 1, p. 367; cf. John Hick, *Philosophy of Religion* (New Jersey: Prentice-Hall, 1973), p. 129
26 Heinz Robert Schlette, *Towards a Theology of Religions* (Montreal: Palm Publishers, Freiburg: Herder, 1966), p. 16
27 Ibid., p. 16
28 See Ibid., p. 17
29 *Vatican Council II: the Conciliar and Post Conciliar Documents*, vol. 1, pp. 738–42
30 Ibid., p. 748
31 Ibid., p. 755
32 Ibid., p. 813
33 Ibid., pp. 824–5
34 Ibid., vol. 2, pp. 719–20
35 Ibid., p. 734
36 Paul Tillich, *The Future of Religions* (New York: Harper & Row, 1966), p. 31
37 Paul Tillich, *Perspectives on Nineteenth and Twentieth Century Protestant Theology* ed. by Carl E. Braaten (London: SCM Press, 1967), p. 213
38 Paul Tillich, *Christianity and the Encounter of the World Religions* (New York: Columbia University Press, 1963), p. 43; *Dynamics of Faith* (New York: Harper, 1957), pp. 12–16; *The Future of Religions*, pp. 80–1; *Perspectives on Nineteenth and Twentieth Century Protestant Theology*, p. xxv
39 Karl Rahner, *Theological Investigations* (New York: Darton, Longman and Todd, 1975), Vol 5; John Hick, *God and the Universe of Faiths* (London: Macmillan, 1973)

2 THE NEO-ORTHODOX RESPONSE

1 Paul Tillich, *The Future of Religions*, p. 81
2 Karl Barth, *Church Dogmatics* vol.I, part 2, ed. by G. W. Bromiley and T. F. Torrance (Edinburgh: T. & T. Clark, 1956), pp. 303f., 325f., 337f., 353f.
3 Ibid., pp. 297–303, 307–10, 325–8, 332–3, 337–8, 353–4
4 Ibid., vol. I, part 1, pp.98–140
5 Ibid., pp. 339–40
6 Ibid., pp. 344–5
7 Ibid., p. 346
8 Ibid., p. 348

9   Ibid., p. 368
10 Ibid., pp. 369, 371
11 Ibid., pp. 441f., 458f., 513f.
12 Emil Brunner, *Revelation and Reason*, trans. by Olive Wyon (London: SCM Press, 1947), p. 43
13 Ibid., p. 8
14 Ibid., pp. 32–5
15 Ibid. pp. 58–61
16 Ibid., p. 62
17 Ibid., p. 76
18 Ibid., p. 77
19 Ibid., p. 220
20 Ibid., p. 225
21 Ibid., p. 236
22 Ibid., p. 258
23 Ibid., p. 264
24 Ibid., p. 270
25 Hendrik Kraemer, *The Christian Message in a Non-Christian World* (London: Edinburgh House Press, 1938), pp. 69–71, 73
26 Ibid., p. 111
27 Ibid., pp. 113–14
28 Ibid., p. 120
29 Ibid., pp. 122–3
30 Ibid., p. 125
31 Hendrik Kraemer, *Why Christianity of all the Religions* (London: Lutterworth Press, 1962), p. 13. Originally published as *Waaram Nu Juist Het Christendom?* (Niyjkerk: G. F. Callenbach, N. V., 1960)
32 Ibid., pp. 41–6
33 Ibid., p. 60
34 Ibid., pp. 64–6
35 Ibid., p. 80
36 Ibid., pp. 94–6
37 Ibid., p. 110
38 Ibid., p. 117

3   THE RESPONSE OF RELATIVISM AND INCLUSIVISM

1   Ernst Troeltsch, 'Historiography', in *Contemporary Religious Thinkers*, ed. by John Macquarrie (New York: Harper & Row, 1968), p.90. The article is reprinted with permission from the *Encyclopedia of Religion and Ethics*, vol. VI, ed. by James Hastings (New York: Charles Scribner, 1913), pp. 716–23
2   Ernst Troeltsch, 'The Place of Christianity Among the World Religions', in *Christian Thought: Its History and Application* (New York: Meridian Books, and London: University of London Press, 1957), pp. 35–63. Quoted from *Attitudes Towards Other Religions*, ed. by Owen C. Thomas (New York: Harper & Row, 1969), p. 73
3   *Attitudes Towards Other Religions*, p. 74

4   Ibid., p. 79
5   Ibid., p. 79
6   Ibid., pp. 80–3
7   Ernst Troeltsch, *The Absoluteness of Christianity and the History of Religions* (London: SCM Press, 1972), p. 41
8   Ibid., pp. 47–8
9   Ibid., p. 49
10 Ibid., p. 57
11 Ibid., p. 64
12 Ibid., pp. 67–70
13 Ibid., p. 71
14 Ibid., p. 76
15 Ibid., pp. 118, 121
16 Ibid., p. 126
17 Ibid., p 131
18 Ibid., p. 86
19 Ibid., p. 86
20 Ibid., pp.87–8
21 Ibid., p. 90
22 Ibid., p. 91
23 Arnold Toynbee, *Christianity Among the Religions of the World* (Oxford: Oxford University Press, 1957), p. vii
24 Ibid., pp. 3–28
25 Ibid., p. 55
26 Ibid., pp. 63–4
27 Ibid., pp. 85–8
28 Ibid., p. 96
29 Ibid., pp. 97–9
30 Ibid., pp. 99–103
31 Ibid., pp. 103–5
32 Ibid., pp. 111–12

4   THE ESSENTIALIST APPROACH

1   Friedrich Schleiermacher, *On Religion: Speeches to its Cultured Despisers* (New York: Harper, 1958), p. 40
2   Ibid., pp. 236, 238
3   Ibid., pp. 251–2
4   Ibid., pp. 15,16
5   Ibid., p. 39
6   Ibid., pp. 48, 49
7   Ibid., p. 38
8   Ibid., pp. 92–101
9   Ibid., p. 101
10 Ibid., pp. 211–13, 217
11 Ibid., pp. 215–17. Cf. Paul Tillich, *The Future of Religions* (New York: Harper & Row, 1966), pp. 86–91, where he insists that the Religion of

the Concrete Spirit which harmonizes the dynamic-typological elements of the holy can be found only in the depths of particular religions.

12 *On Religion: Speeches to its Cultured Despisers*, pp. 213, 217–8, 224–5
13 Ibid., pp. 214, 224–5
14 Ibid., pp.227, 245, 247, 249
15 Ibid., pp. 251–2
16 Friedrich Schleieirmacher, *The Christian Faith* (Edinburgh: T. & T. Clark, 1928, 1948, 1956), p. 12
17 Wilfred Cantwell Smith, *Towards a World Theology* (London: Macmillan, 1981), p. 114
18 Ibid., p. 117
19 *The Christian Faith*, p. 33
20 Ibid., p. 38
21 Ibid., p. 52
22 Ibid., pp. 62–5
23 Ibid., pp. 131, 133
24 Ibid., pp. 385–7
25 Ibid., pp. 361, 371
26 Ibid., p. 377
27 Ibid., p. 387
28 Ibid., p. 388
29 *On Religion: Speeches to its Cultured Despisers*, p. 252
30 William Ernest Hocking, *Living Religions and a World Faith* (New York: Macmillan, 1940), p. 8
31 Ibid., p. 21
32 Ibid., pp. 26–9
33 Ibid., p. 32
34 Ibid., p. 43
35 Ibid., pp. 47–59
36 Ibid., p. 77
37 Ibid., pp. 100–2
38 Ibid., p. 116
39 Ibid., pp. 190–208; cf. Owen C. Thomas, *Attitudes Towards Other Religions* (New York: Harper & Row, 1969), pp. 135–49
40 See above p. 36
41 John Macquarrie, *20th Century Religious Thought* (London: SCM Press, 1963), pp. 48–9
42 Rudolf Otto, *The Idea of the Holy* (New York: Oxford University Press, 1958), p. 4
43 Ibid., p.7
44 Ibid., pp. 12–19
45 Ibid., pp. 19–23
46 Ibid., pp. 23–4
47 Ibid., p. 31
48 William J. Wainwright, 'Rudolf Otto', in *The Encyclopedia of Philosophy*, ed. by Paul Edwards, vol. 6 (New York: Macmillan, 1967), pp. 13–15
49 See *20th Century Religious Thought*, pp. 213–16

50 *The Idea of the Holy*, p. 113
51 Carl Gustav Jung, *Modern Man in Search of a Soul* (London: Kegan Paul, 1933), p. 264 (New York: Harcourt, Brace & World, Inc., 1933). See John Macquarrie, *Contemporary Religious Thinkers* (New York: Harper & Row, 1968), p. 109
52 The Collected Works of C. G. Jung, vol. 12, *Psychology and Alchemy* (London: Routledge & Kegan Paul, 1968), p. 4
53 Ibid., pp. 277–82. See *Contemporary Religious Thinkers*, pp. 128–32
54 Alistair MacIntyre, 'Carl Gustav Jung', in *Encyclopedia of Philosophy*, vol. 4 (New York: Macmillan, 1967), p. 296
55 *The Collected Works of C. G. Jung*, vol. 7, *Two Essays on Analytical Psychology* (London: Routledge & Kegan Paul, 1953), p. 65
56 *Collected Works of C. G. Jung*, vol. 12, p. 11
57 Ibid., p. 12
58 Ibid., p. 14
59 Ibid., p. 18
60 *Modern Man in Search of a Soul*, p. 282. See *Contemporary Religious Thinkers*, p. 132
61 Carl Gustav Jung, *Psychology and Religion* (New Haven: Yale University Press, 1938), pp. 6, 7
62 Ibid., p. 52
63 *Collected Works of C. G. Jung*, vol. 12, p. 17
64 Ibid., p. 18
65 Ibid., pp. 19–20
66 Ibid., p. 17

5 THE CATHOLIC RESPONSE

1 Sarvepalli Radhakrishnan, *Eastern Religions and Western Thought* (New York and London: Oxford University Press, 1940), pp. 308, 313; N.K. Bose, *Selections from Gandhi* (Ahmedabad: Navajivan Publishing House, 1948), p. 256; Glyn Richards, *The Philosophy of Gandhi* (London: Curzon Press, 1982), p. 20
2 Denzinger, H. J. D., *Enchiridion*, (ed. by Karl Rahner (Freiberg, 1955), pp. 468f. quoted in Owen C. Thomas, *Attitudes Towards Other Religions* (New York: Harper & Row, 1969), p. 195
3 Hans Kung, *Freedom Today* (New York: Sheed & Ward, 1966), pp. 110–24; cf. *Attitudes Towards Other Religions*, pp. 193–9; cf. Hans Kung, *On Being a Christian* (London: Collins, Fount Paperback, 1978), pp. 89–91
4 De Ecclesia ii, 16; cf. *Attitudes Towards Other Religions*, p. 202
5 Cf. *Attitudes Towards Other Religions*, p. 206
6 Cf. J. Neuner, 'Missionstheologische Probleme in Indien', in *Gott in Welt. Festgabe Für Karl Rahner* (ed. by Johannes Baptist Metz) (Freiburg, Basel, Vienna, 1964), pp. 401f.
7 H. R. Schlette, *Towards a Theology of Religions* (Montreal: Palm Publishers; Freiburg: Herder, 1966), p. 37

8   Cf. *Attitudes Towards Other Religions*, pp. 210–13
9   Ibid., pp. 215–17; *Freedom Today*, pp. 132–45, 147–60; cf. *On Being a Christian*, pp. 111–12
10 *On Being a Christian*, p. 98
11 Ibid., p. 98
12 Ibid., pp. 99, 104
13 Ibid., p. 104
14 See note 7
15 *Towards a Theology of Religions*, p. 9
16 Ibid., pp. 67, 69
17 Ibid., p.78
18 Ibid., p. 104
19 Ibid., p.104
20 Ibid., pp. 30, 34–36, 105
21 Ibid., pp. 115, 118
22 'Christianity and the Non-Christian Religions', in Karl Rahner, *Theological Investigations*, vol. 5 (London: Darton, Longman & Todd, 1966), p. 115
23 Ibid., p. 117
24 Ibid., p. 119
25 Ibid., p. 125
26 Ibid., pp. 128–9
27 Ibid., pp. 131–2
28 The terms 'anonymous Christian' and 'anonymous Christianity' are criticized on the grounds that they are irreconcilable with the doctrine of the missionary task of the Church. Rahner rejects these criticisms, claiming that what the terms signify is 'nothing else than the fact that according to the doctrine of the Church herself an individual can already be in possession of sanctifying grace, can in other words be justified and sanctified, a child of God, an heir to heaven, positively oriented by grace towards his supernatural and eternal salvation even before he has explicitly embraced a credal statement of the Christian faith and been baptized.' Furthermore, the missionary task of the Church is reconcilable with anonymous Christianity, he claims, because it 'presupposes the existence of the anonymous Christian as the only possible hearer of the gospel message'. 'Anonymous Christianity and the Missionary Task of the Church', in *Theological Investigations*, vol. 12 (London: Darton Longman & Todd, 1966), pp. 165, 171
29 Ibid., pp. 133–4
30 Ibid., p. 115

6   THE DYNAMIC-TYPOLOGICAL APPROACH

1   Paul Tillich, *The Future of Religions*, ed. by Jerald C. Brauer (New York: Harper & Row, 1966), pp. 80, 93
2   Paul Tillich, *Systematic Theology*, vol. 3 (London: Nisbet, 1968), p. 395
3   Ibid., p. 389

4   Ibid., p. 393;
5   D. M. Baillie, *God was in Christ* (London: Faber & Faber, 1948), p. 76
6   For a fuller treatment of Tillich's view of the historical Jesus see my article 'Paul Tillich and the Historical Jesus', *Studies in Religion*, vol.4, no. 2, (1974–5), pp. 120–8
7   *The Future of Religions*, pp. 86–7
8   Paul Tillich, *Perspectives on Nineteenth and Twentieth Century Protestant Theology*, ed. by Carl E. Braaten (London: SCM Press, 1967), p. xxv
9   *The Future of Religions*, pp. 86–91
10 Ibid., p. 86
11 Paul Tillich, *Christianity and the Encounter of the World Religions* (New York: Columbia University Press, 1963), pp. 54–5
12 *The Future of Religions*, p. 88
13 Ibid., p. 88
14 Mircea Eliade, 'Paul Tillich and the History of Religions', in *The Future of Religions*, p. 32
15 Ibid., pp. 32–3
16 Ibid., p. 35
17 Ibid., p. 33
18 Ibid., p. 35
19 *Christianity and the Encounter of the World Religions*, p. 44
20 Ibid., p. 45; see also Paul Tillich, *Ultimate Concern: Tillich in Dialogue* (New York: Harper & Row, 1965), p. 63
21 Ibid., pp. 44–6: see also Paul Tillich, *The Protestant Era* (Chicago: University of Chicago Press, 1948), p. 62 and *The Future of Religions*, p. 80
22 Ibid., pp. 41–2
23 Ibid., p. 54
24 Ibid., p. 57
25 Ibid., pp. 57–8
26 Ibid., p. 62
27 Ibid., pp. 65–6
28 Ibid., p. 68
29 Ibid., p. 69
30 Ibid., pp. 71–2
31 Paul Tillich, *The Shaking of the Foundations* (London: Pelican, 1962), pp. 163–4; Paul Tillich, *The Courage to Be* (London: Nisbet, 1952), p. 39
32 *Christianity and the Encounter of the World Religions*, p. 72
33 *Systematic Theology*, vol 3, p. 375
34 *Christianity and the Encounter of the World Religions*, p. 73
35 Ibid., pp. 73–5
36 Ibid., p. 95

7   THE DIALOGICAL APPROACH

1   John Hick, *God and the Universe of Faiths* (Glasgow: Collins, 1977), pp. viii, ix. First published by Macmillan, 1973

2   Ibid., p. xv
3   Ibid., p. 148
4   Ibid., p. 165
5   Ibid., p. 167
6   Ibid., p. 172
7   Ibid., pp. 172–7
8   Ibid., p. 177
9   Ibid., pp. 133–47
10 Ibid., pp. 138–9
11 Ibid., p. 146
12 John Hick, *God Has Many Names* (London: Macmillan, 1980), pp. 8f., 58f., 61f., 81f
13 'The Outcome: Dialogue into Truth', in *Truth and Dialogue*, ed. by John Hick (London: Sheldon Press, 1974)
14 Op. cit., p. 140
15 Op. cit., p. 142
16 John Hick, 'On Grading Religions', *Religious Studies* 17:4,(1981), pp. 451–67. A reply to Hick's article by Paul Griffiths and Delmas Lewis appeared in *Religious Studies* 19:1, (1983) pp. 75–80; it argued that criteria must be developed wherby competing religious views can be assessed. Cf. Hick's rejoinder 'On Conflicting Religious Truth Claims', *Religious Studies* 19:4 (1983) pp. 485–91. See also Keith Yandell, 'Religious Experience and Rational Appraisal', *Religious Studies* 10:2, (1974), 173–87, in which the self-authenticating nature of religious experience is questioned, and reference is made to the fact that logically inconsistent propositions, and contradiction of well established data, point to a false conceptual system
17 Maurice Wiles, 'Christianity without Incarnation', in *The Myth of God Incarnate*, ed. by John Hick (London: SCM Press, 1977), p. 2. See John Hick, 'Jesus and the World Religions', in *The Myth of God Incarnate*, p. 168
18 *The Myth of God Incarnate*, p. ix
19 'Jesus and the World Religions', in *The Myth of God Incarnate*, p. 180
20 Ibid., p. 181
21 J. A. T. Robinson, *Truth is Two-Eyed* (London: SCM Press, 1979), pp. ix, x
22 Ibid., p. 4
23 Ibid., p. 17
24 Hugo Meynell, 'Towards a New Dialectic of Religions', *Religious Studies* 18:4, (1982), 417–31
25 Ninian Smart, *A Dialogue of Religions* (London: SCM Press, 1960), p. 9
26 Ibid., pp. 9, 11
27 Ibid., pp. 12–13
28 Ibid., pp. 17–130 *passim*
29 Ninian Smart, *Reasons and Faiths* (London: Routledge & Kegan Paul, 1958)
30 Cf. 'Truth and Religions', in *Truth and Dialogue*, p. 45
31 *Reasons and Faiths*, p. 7

32 Ibid., p. 197
33 Ibid., pp. 198–200
34 *Truth and Dialogue*, pp. 47–9
35 Ibid., p. 52
36 Ibid., p. 53
37 Ibid., pp. 54–57
38 Wilfred Cantwell Smith, 'Comparative Religion: Whither – and Why?', in *The History of Religions: Essays in Methodology*, ed. by Mircea Eliade and Joseph M. Kitagawa, pp. 34–55 *passim*
39 Wilfred Cantwell Smith, *Towards a World Theology* (London: Macmillan, 1981), pp. 152, 168
40 Wilfred Cantwell Smith, *The Meaning and End of Religion* (New York: Mentor, 1964), pp. 114, 141, 162, 175, 309–10
41 Wilfred Cantwell Smith, 'A Human View of Truth', *Truth and Dialogue*, pp. 20–44;
42 Wilfred Cantwell Smith, 'Conflicting Truth-Claims: Rejoinder', *Truth and Dialogue*, pp. 156–62
43 Wilfred Cantwell Smith, 'Comparative Religion: Whither – and Why?', in *The History of Religions: Essays in Methodology*, pp. 42, 55
44 Wilfred Cantwell Smith, *The Faith of Other Men* (New York: Harper Torchbooks, 1972), pp. 98–139 *passim*
45 Raimundo Panikkar, *The Intra-Religious Dialogue* (New York: Paulist Press, 1978), p. xxvii
46 Ibid., p. 8
47 Ibid., p. 12
48 Ibid., p. 16
49 Ibid., p. 22
50 Ibid., pp. 26–30
51 Ibid., p. 31
52 Peter Winch, 'Understanding a Primitive Society', in *Religion and Understanding*, ed. by D. Z. Phillips (Oxford: Blackwell, 1967), p. 30
53 *The Intra-Religious Dialogue*, pp. 31–2
54 Ibid., pp. 41–2
55 Ibid., p. 52
56 Ibid., p. 54
57 Ibid., p. 72
58 Ibid., p. 73
59 Raimundo Pannikar, *The Unknown Christ of Hinduism* (New York: Orbis Books, 1981), p. 1. Originally published by Darton, Longman & Todd, London, 1964
60 Ibid., p. 7
61 Ibid., pp. 9, 11
62 Ibid., p. 12
63 Ibid., pp. 25, 27
64 Ibid., pp. 23, 30

8 THE CHRISTOCENTRIC RESPONSE

1 M. M. Thomas, *Man and the Universe of Faiths* (Madras: Christian Literature Society, 1975, p. xiii
2 Ibid., pp. 32–4
3 Ibid., pp. 151–2
4 Visser't Hooft, *No Other Name* (London: SCM Press, 1963), pp. 96–7, 116, 125
5 Op. cit., p. 157
6 M. M. Thomas, *The Acknowledged Christ of the Indian Renaissance* (London: SCM Press, 1969), pp. x, 284
7 Ibid., pp. 300–1
8 Ibid., p. 308
9 Ibid., p. 316
10 Paul Devanandan, *The Gospel and Renascent Hinduism* (London: SCM Press, 1959)
11 *Preparation for Dialogue*, ed. by Nalini Devanandan and M. M. Thomas (Bangalore: CISRS, 1964), p. 167
12 Stanley J. Samartha, *The Hindu Response to the Unbound Christ* (Madras: Christian Literature Society, 1974)
13 Ibid., pp. 3, 6–7
14 Ibid., pp. 10–17
15 Ibid., pp. 19–115 *passim*
16 Ibid., pp. 116–21
17 Ibid., pp. 122–4
18 Ibid., pp. 129–30. See A. J. Appasamy, *Christianity as Bhakti Marga* (Madras: Christian Literature Society, 1928)
19 *The Hindu Response to the Unbound Christ*, p. 131. See V. Chakkarai, *Jesus the Avatar* (Madras: Christian Literature Society, 1930)
20 *The Hindu Response to the Unbound Christ*, pp. 131–3. See P. Chenchiah, *Rethinking Christianity in India* (Madras: A. N. Sudarshanam, 1939)
21 *The Hindu Response to the Unbound Christ*, pp. 139–41. See Raimundo Panikkar, *The Unknown Christ of Hinduism* (London: Darton, Longman & Todd, 1964 and New York: Orbis Books, 1981)
22 *The Hindu Response to the Unbound Christ*, p. 147
23 Ibid., pp. 154, 159f
24 Ibid., pp. 162–7
25 Ibid., p.171
26 Stanley J. Samartha, *Courage for Dialogue* (New York: Orbis Books, 1982)
27 Ibid., p. 12
28 Ibid., pp. 33–4
29 Ibid., p. 43
30 Ibid., p. 59
31 Ibid., p. 68
32 Ibid., p. 97
33 Ibid., pp. 98–9

9 THE SEARCH FOR INDEPENDENT
CRITERIA OF TRUTH

1   D.Z. Phillips, *Faith and Philosophical Enquiry* (London: Routlege, 1970), pp. 85–92, 101
2   Cf. D.Z. Phillips's review of Ninian Smart's, *The Phenomenon of Religion* (London: Macmillan, 1973), in *Mind* , vol. lxxxiv, no. 333, January, 1975, pp. 155–6
3   Peter Winch, 'Understanding a Primitive Society', *Religion and Understanding*, ed. by D.Z. Phillips (Oxford: Blackwell, 1967), p. 30
4   See above p. 41
5   See above p. 55
6   See above p. 8
7   See above p. 29
8   Cf. D.Z. Phillips, *Religion without Explanatiom* (Oxford: Blackwell, 1976), pp. 1–3; *Faith and Philosophical Enquiry* (London: Routledge, 1965), p. 125; *Concept of Prayer*, London: Routledge, 1965), p. 12
9   L. Wittgenstein, *Lectures and Conversation on Aesthetics, Psychology, and Religious Belief*, ed. by C. Barrett (Oxford: Blackwell, 1966), p. 72
10   *Religion without Explanation*, p. 172
11   Rush Rhees, 'Some Developments in Wittgenstein's View of Ethics', in *Discussions of Wittgenstein*, ed. by D.Z. Phillips (London: Routledge, 1970), pp. 131–2
12   *Lectures and Conversations on Aesthetics, Psychology and Religious Belief*, p. 59
13   *Religion without Explanation*, p. 172
14   Ibid., p. 181
15   D.Z. Phillips, *Athronyddu am Grefydd* (Llandysul: Gwasg Gomer, 1974), p. 91
16   This is an accusation levelled against Barth by Dietrich Bonhoeffer. Cf. Dietrich Bonhoeffer, *Letters and Papers from Prison* (London and Glasgow: Collins, Fontana, 1963), p. 95, where Bonhoeffer states: 'Barth was the first theologian to begin the criticism of religion – and that remains his really great merit – but he set in its place the positivist doctrine of revelation which says in effect, "Take it or leave it". . . .That is not in accordance with the Bible.'

10   AN ASSESSMENT OF RESPONSES TO PLURALITY

1   *Light of Truth or An English Translation of the Satyarth Prakash*, by Dayananda Saraswati, translated by Chirandjiva Bharadwaya (New Delhi: Sarvadeshik Arya Pratinidhi Sabha, 1975), p. 723
2   Ibid., p. 75
3   Ibid., p. 372
4   Ibid., p. 219
5   Ibid., p. 373
6   Ibid., pp. 383–4
7   *The Complete Works of Swami Vivekananda*, vol. III (Calcutta: Advaita Ashrama, 1970), p. 278–80

8   Ibid., p. 278-80
9   Ibid., vol.I, p. 388
10 Ibid., p. 375
11 Ibid., vol. VII, p. 101
12 Ibid., vol.I, p. 356
13 Ibid., vol. II, p. 133
14 Ibid., pp. 254, 334, 381
15 Ibid., p. 253
16 Swami Vivekananda, *Addresses on Vedanta Philosophy*, vol. II, *Bhakti Yoga* (London: Simkin Marshall, Hamilton, Kent and Co., 1896), p. 65, quoted from *Modern Indian Responses to Religious Pluralism*, ed. by Harold G. Coward (Albany: SUNY, 1987), p. 77
17 Swami Vivekananda, *Religion of Love* (Belur: Ramakrishna Math, 1927), p. 24
18 S. Radhakrishnan, *An Idealist View of Life* (London: George Allen & Unwin, 1961), pp. 69–70
19 S. Radhakrishnan, *The Hindu Way of Life* (London: George Allen & Unwin, 1964), p. 129
20 S. Radhakrishnan, *Indian Religions* (New Delhi: Vision Books, 1979), p. 13
21 S. Radhakrishnan, *Eastern Religions and Western Thought* (Oxford: Oxford University Press, 1940), p. 347
22 S. Radhakrishnan, *Recovery of Faith* (New York: Harper, 1955), p. 157
23 M. K. Gandhi, *All Men Are Brothers* ed. by Krishna Kripalani (Unesco, 1958, 1969), pp. 56, 59
24 N. K. Bose (ed.), *Selections from Gandhi* (Ahmedabad: Navajivan Publishing House, 1948), p. 257
25 Ibid., p. 256
26 Ibid., p. 259
27 M. K. Gandhi, *In Search of the Supreme*, vol. 3 (Ahmedabad: Navajivan Publishing House, 1931), p. 54
28 *Keshub Chunder Sen's Lectures in India* (London: Cassell, 1901), p. 133
29 *The Gospel of Sri Ramakrishna*, originally recorded in Bengali by M. (Mahendranath Gupta), translated by Swami Nikhilananda (Madras: Sri Ramakrishna Math, Mylapore, 1969), p. 204
30 M. K. Gandhi, *Truth is God*, compiled by R. K. Prabhu (Ahmedabad: Navajivan Publishing House, 1955, 1969), pp. 11–12
31 N. Pyarelal, *Mahatma Gandhi, The Early Phase*, vol. I (Ahmedabad: Navajivan Publishing House, 1965), p. 277
32 See J. F. T. Jorden, 'Gandhi and Religious Pluralism', in *Modern Indian Responses to Religious Pluralism*, ed. by Harold G. Coward (Albany: SUNY, 1987), pp. 3–17; Glyn Richards, *The Philosophy of Gandhi*, chap. I (London and Dublin: Curzon Press, 1982)

BIBLIOGRAPHY

BOOKS

Appasamy, A. J. *Christianity as Bhakti Marga*, Madras: Christian Literature Society, 1928

Baillie, D. M. *God was in Christ*, London: Faber & Faber, 1948

Barth, Karl *Church Dogmatics* vol.I, parts 1, 2, ed.by G. W. Bromiley and T. F. Torrance, Edinburgh: T. & T. Clark, 1956

Bonhoeffer, Dietrich *Letters and Papers from Prison*, London and Glasgow: Collins, Fontana, 1963

Brunner, Emil *Revelation and Reason*, trans. by Olive Wyon. London: SCM Press, 1947

Bose, N. K. (ed.) *Selections from Gandhi*, Ahmedabad: Navajivan Publishing House, 1948

Chakkarai, V. *Jesus the Avatar*, Madras: Christian Literature Society, 1930

Chenchiah, P. *Rethinking Christianity in India*, Madras: A. N. Sudarshanam, 1939

Clayton, John Powell, (ed.) *Ernst Troeltsch and the Future of Theology*, Cambridge: Cambridge University Press, 1976

Coward, Harold G. *Pluralism: Challenge to World Religions*, New York: Orbis Books, 1985

Coward, Harold G. (ed.) *Modern Indian Responses to Religious Pluralism*, Albany: SUNY Press, 1987

D'Costa, Gavin *Theology and Religious Pluralism*, Oxford: Blackwell, 1986

Devanandan, Paul *The Gospel and Renascent Hinduism*, London: SCM Press, 1959

Devanandan Nalini and Thomas, M. M. (eds) *Preparation for Dialogue*, Bangalore: CISRS, 1964

Edwards, Paul (ed.) *The Encyclopedia of Philosophy*, vols. 3,4,6, New York: Macmillan, 1967

Eliade, Mircea and Kitagawa, Joseph M. (eds) *The History of Religions: Essays in Methodology*, Chicago: University of Chicago Press, 1959

Gandhi, M. K. *In Search of the Supreme*, Ahmedabad: Navajivan Publishing House, 1931

Gandhi, M. K. *Truth is God*, compiled by R. K. Prabhu, Ahmedabad: Navajivan Publishing House, 1955, 1969

Gandhi, M. K. *All Men Are Brothers*, ed. by Krishna Kripalani, Paris: Unesco, 1958, 1969

Hasting, James (ed.) *Encyclopedia of Religion and Ethics*, vol. VI, New York: Charles Scribner, 1913.

Hick, John *Philosophy of Religion*, New Jersey: Prentice-Hall, 1973

Hick, John *God and the Universe of Faiths*, London: MacMillan, 1973; Glasgow: Collins, 1977

Hick, John (ed.) *Truth and Dialogue*, London: Sheldon Press, 1974

Hick, John (ed.) *The Myth of God Incarnate*, London: SCM Press, 1977

Hick, John *God Has Many Names*, London: Macmillan, 1980

Hick, John *Problems of Religious Pluralism*, London: Macmillan, 1985

Hick, John and Hebblethwiate, Brian *Christianity and Other Religions*, Philadelphia: Fortress Press, 1981

Hocking, William Ernest *Living Religions and a World Faith*, New York: Macmillan, 1940

Hocking, William Ernest *The Meaning of God in Human Experience*, New Haven: Yale University Press, 1944

Jung, Carl Gustav *Modern Man in Search of a Soul*, London: Kegan Paul, 1933, New York: Harcourt, Brace & World, Inc., 1933

Jung, Carl Gustav *Psychology and Religion*, New Haven: Yale University Press, 1938

Jung, Carl Gustav *The Collected Works of C. G. Jung*, vol. 7 *Two Essays on Analytical Psychology*, London: Routledge & Kegan Paul, 1953

Jung, Carl Gustav *The Collected Works of C. G. Jung*, vol. 12 *Psychology and Alchemy*, London: Routledge & Kegan Paul, 1968

Knitter, Paul F. *No Other Name*, New York: Orbis Books, 1985

Kraemer, Hendrik *The Christian Message in a Non-Christian World*, London: Edinburgh House Press, 1938

Kraemer, Hendrik *Why Christianity of all the Religions*, London: Lutterworth Press, 1962. Originally published as *Waaram Nu Juist Het Christendom?*, Niyjkerk: G. F. Callenbach, N. V., 1960

Kung, Hans *Freedom Today*, New York: Sheed & Ward, 1966

Kung, Hans *On Being a Christian*, London: Collins, Fount Paperback, 1978

Kung, Hans and Moltmann, Jurgen *Christianity Among World Religions*, Edinburgh: T. & T. Clark, 1986

Klostermaier, Klaus *Liberation-Salvation-Self-Realization*, Madras: University of Madras, 1973

Lewis, H. D. and Slater, Robert Lawson *The Study of Religions*, London: Penguin Books, 1969

Macquarrie, John *20th Century Religious Thought*, London: SCM Press, 1963

Macquarrie, John (ed.) *Contemporary Religious Thinkers*, New York: Harper & Row, 1968

Otto, Rudolf *The Idea of the Holy*, New York: Oxford University Press, 1958

Panikkar, Raimundo *The Unknown Christ of Hinduism*, New York: Orbis Books, 1981. Originally published by Darton, Longman & Todd, London, in 1964

Panikkar, Raimundo *The Intra-Religious Dialogue*, New York: Paulist Press, 1978

Phillips, D. Z. *Concept of Prayer*, London: Routledge, 1965
Phillips, D. Z. (ed.) *Religion and Understanding*, Oxford: Blackwell, 1967
Phillips, D. Z. *Faith and Philosophical Enquiry*, London: Routlege, 1965
Phillips, D. Z. (ed.) *Discussions of Wittgenstein*, London: Routledge, 1970
Phillips, D. Z. *Athronyddu am Grefydd*, Llandysul: Gwasg Gomer, 1974
Phillips, D. Z. *Religion without Explanation*, Oxford: Blackwell, 1976
Pyarelal, N. *Mahatma Gandhi, The Early Phase*, Ahmedabad: Navajivan
   Publishing House, 1965
Race, Alan *Christians and Religious Pluralism*, London: SCM Press, 1983
Radhakrishnan, S. *Eastern Religions and Western Thought*, Oxford: Oxford
   University Press, 1940
Radhakrishnan, S. *Recovery of Faith*, New York: Harper, 1955
Radhakrishnan, S. *An Idealist View of Life*, London: George Allen &
   Unwin, 1961
Radhakrishnan, S. *The Hindu Way of Life*, London: George Allen & Unwin,
   1964
Radhakrishnan, S. *Indian Religions*, New Delhi: Vision Books, 1979
Rahner, Karl *Theological Investigations*, vols. 5, 12, New York: Darton,
   Longman & Todd, 1966.
The Gospel of Sri Ramakrishna, originally recorded in Bengali by M.
   (Mahendranath Gupta), trans. by Swami Nikhilananda, Madras: Sri
   Ramakrishna Math, Mylapore, 1969
Richards, Glyn *The Philosophy of Gandhi*, London and Dublin: Curzon
   Press, 1982
Richards, Glyn *A Source-Book of Modern Hinduism*, London: Curzon Press,
   1985
Robinson, J. A. T. *Truth is Two-Eyed*, London: SCM Press, 1979
Russell, Bertrand *A History of Western Philosophy*, London: George Allen &
   Unwin, 1946
Samartha, Stanley J. *Courage for Dialogue*, New York: Orbis Books, 1982
Samartha, Stanley J. *The Hindu Response to the Unbound Christ*, Madras:
   Christian Literature Society, 1974
Saraswati, Dayananda *Light of Truth or An English Translation of the Satyarth
   Prakash*, Trans. by Chirandjiva Bharadwaya, New Delhi: Sarvadeshik
   Arya Pratinidhi Sabha, 1975
Schleieirmacher, Friedrich *The Christian Faith*, Edinburgh: T. & T. Clark,
   1928, 1948, 1956
Schleiermacher, Friedrich *On Religion: Speeches to its Cultured Despisers*, New
   York: Harper, 1958
Schlette, H. R. *Towards a Theology of Religions*, Montreal: Palm Publishers,
   Freiburg: Herder, 1966
Keshub Chunder Sen's Lectures in India, London: Cassell, 1901
Smart, Ninian *Philosophers and Religious Truth*, London: SCM Press, 1964
Smart, Ninian *The Science of Religion and the Sociology of Knowledge*, Princeton:
   Princeton University Press, 1973
Smart, Ninian *A Dialogue of Religions*, London: SCM Press, 1960
Smart, Ninian *Reasons and Faiths*, London: Routledge & Kegan Paul, 1958
Smart, Ninian *The Phenomenon of Religion*, London: Macmillan, 1973

Smart, Ninian *Concept and Empathy: Essays in the Study of Religion*, ed. by
Donald Wiebe, London: Macmillan, 1986

Smart, Ninian *Beyond Ideology*, London: Collins, 1981

Smith, Wilfred Cantwell *The Faith of Other Men*, New York: Harper
Torchbooks, 1972

Smith, Wilfred Cantwell *Towards a World Theology*, London: Macmillan,
1981

Smith, Wilfred Cantwell *The Meaning and End of Religion*, New York:
Mentor, 1964

Smith, Wilfred Cantwell *Faith and Belief*, Princeton: Princeton University
Press, 1979

Thomas, M. M. *Man and the Universe of Faiths*, Madras: Christian
Literature Society, 1975

Thomas, M. M. *The Acknowledged Christ of the Indian Renaissance*, London:
SCM Press, 1969

Thomas, Owen C. *Attitudes Towards Other Religions*, New York: Harper &
Row, 1969

Tillich, Paul *Christianity and the Encounter of the World Religions*, New York:
Columbia University Press, 1963

Tillich, Paul *Ultimate Concern: Tillich in Dialogue*, New York: Harper &
Row, 1965

Tillich, Paul *The Protestant Era*, Chicago: University of Chicago Press, 1948

Tillich, Paul *The Shaking of the Foundations*, London: Penguin Books, 1962

Tillich, Paul *The Courage to Be*, London: Nisbet, 1952

Tillich, Paul *Systematic Theology*, Vols 1–3. London: Nisbet, 1968

Tillich, Paul *The Future of Religions*, ed. by Jerald C Brauer, New York:
Harper & Row, 1966

Tillich, Paul *Perspectives on Nineteenth and Twentieth Century Protestant Theology*,
ed. by Carl E. Braaten, London: SCM Press, 1967

Tillich, Paul *Dynamics of Faith*, New York: Harper, 1957

Toynbee, Arnold *Christianity Among the Religions of the World*, Oxford:
Oxford University Press, 1957

Troeltsch, Ernst *The Absoluteness of Christianity and the History of Religions*,
London: SCM Press, 1972

Vatican Council II: the Conciliar and Post Conciliar Documents, general editor
Austin Flannery, New York: Costello Publishing Company, 1975, 1984

Visser't Hooft, *No Other Name*, London: SCM Press, 1963

The Complete Works of Swami Vivekananda, vols I, II, III, VII Calcutta:
Advaita Ashrama, 1970

Swami Vivekananda, *Addresses on Vedanta Philosophy*, vol. II, *Bhakti Yoga*,
London: Simkin Marshall, Hamilton, Kent & Co., 1896

Swami Vivekananda, *Religion of Love*. Belur: Ramakrishna Math, 1927

Whaling, Frank (ed.) *The World's Religious Traditions*, Edinburgh: T. & T.
Clark, 1984

Whaling, Frank *Christian Theology and World Religions: A Global Approach*,
Basingstoke: Marshall Pickering, 1986

Wittgenstein, L. *Lectures and Conversation on Aesthetics, Psychology, and Religious
Belief*, ed. by C. Barrett, Oxford: Blackwell, 1966

ARTICLES

Acton, H. B. 'Georg Wilhelm Friedrich Hegel', in *The Encyclopedia of Philosophy*, vols 3, 4 (New York: Macmillan, 1967)

Griffiths, Paul and Lewis, Delmas 'A Reply to Hick On Grading Religions', *Religious Studies* 19:1, 1983, pp.75–80

Hick, John 'On Grading Religions', *Religious Studies* 17:4, 1981, pp.451–67

Hick, John 'On Conflicting Religious Truth Claims', *Religious Studies* 19:4, 1983, pp.485–91

Hick, John 'Jesus and the World Religions', in *The Myth of God Incarnate*, ed. by John Hick, London: SCM Press, 1977

Kitagawa, Joseph M. 'The History of Religions in America', *The History of Religions: Essays in Methodology*, ed. by Mircea Eliade and Joseph M. Kitagawa, Chicago: University of Chicago Press, 1959

Macquarrie, John 'Christianity and Other Faiths', *Union Seminary Quarterly Review*, November 1964, vol. XX, no. 1, pp.39–48. See also the article entitled 'Discussion: Christianity and Other Faiths', vol. XX, no. 2, pp.177–187, which has contributions by Tillich, Roger L. Shinn, Seymor Siegel, and Paul Lehmann and a reply by Macquarrie, pp.188–9

Meynell, Hugo 'Towards a New Dialectic of Religions', *Religious Studies* 18:4, 1982, pp.417–31

Phillips, D. Z. review of Ninian Smart's *The Phenomenon of Religion*, in *Mind*, vol. lxxxiv, no. 333, January 1975

Rhees, Rush 'Some Developments in Wittgenstein's View of Ethics', *Discussions of Wittgenstein*, ed. by D. Z. Phillips, London: Routledge, 1970

Richards, Glyn 'Paul Tillich and the Historical Jesus', *Studies in Religion* vol. 4, no. 2, 1974–5, pp. 120–8

Richards, Glyn 'Towards a Theology of Religions', *The Journal of Theological Studies*, vol. XXXI, part I, April 1980, pp. 46–66

Smart, Ninian 'Truth and Religions', in *Truth and Dialogue*, ed. by John Hick, London: Sheldon Press, 1974

Smith, Wilfred Cantwell 'A Human View of Truth', in *Truth and Dialogue*, ed. by John Hick, London: Sheldon Press, 1974.

Smith, Wilfred Cantwell 'Conflicting Truth-Claims: Rejoinder', in *Truth and Dialogue*, ed. by John Hick, London: Sheldon Press, 1974

Smith, Wilfred Cantwell, 'Comparative Religion: Whither – and Why?', in *The History of Religions: Essays in Methodology*, ed. by Mircea Eliade and Joseph M. Kitagawa, Chicago: University of Chicago Press, 1959

Tillich, Paul 'A Reinterpretation of the Doctrine of the Incarnation', *Church Quarterly Review*, CXLVII, no. 294, 1949, pp.133–48

Tillich, Paul 'What is Wrong with the "Dialectic" Theology', *Journal of Religion*, vol. XV, no. 2, April 1935, pp.127–45

Wiebe, Don 'A Positive Episteme for the Study of Religion', *The Scottish Journal of Religious Studies*, vol.VI, 2, Autumn 1985

Wiles, Maurice 'Christianity without Incarnation', in *The Myth of God Incarnate*, ed. by John Hick, London: SCM Press, 1977

Winch, Peter 'Understanding a Primitive Society', *Religion and Understanding*, ed. by D.Z. Phillips, Oxford: Blackwell, 1967

Yandell, Keith 'Religious Experience and Rational Appraisal', *Religious Studies* 10:2, pp.173–87

INDEX